H I LOVE TO
OWN KINKAID
TO THEE I BRING
OWN KINKAID
OYALTY AND CHEER
LEDGE FAR AND NEAR
CEPTS EVER DEAR
OWN KINKAID

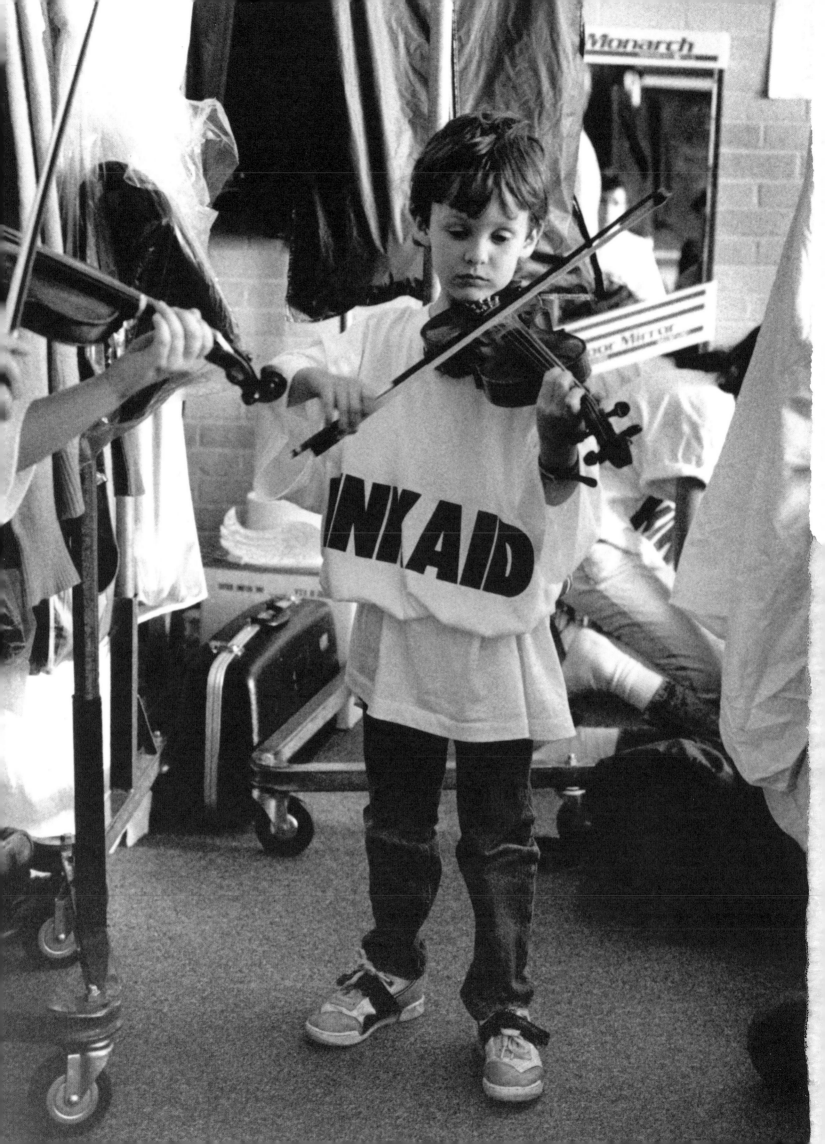

# THE KINKAID SCHOOL

*A Legacy of Distinction ~ The First 100 Years*

Published in the United States by
The Kinkaid School
201 Kinkaid School Drive
Houston, Texas 77024

In the making of this book, every attempt has been made to verify names, facts and figures.

ISBN  0-9772854-0-5

Printed in the United States of America by
Grover Printing, a Consolidated Graphics Company

*A Legacy of Distinction: The First 100 Years* is a charitable project. All net proceeds will benefit The Kinkaid School, Inc., a 501(c)(3) non-profit corporation.

Any inquiries about this book or orders for additional copies should be directed to:

The Kinkaid School
Alumni / Development Office
201 Kinkaid School Drive
Houston, Texas  77024

713-782-1640
www.kinkaid.org

First Edition

### PRINTING

The Kinkaid School acknowledges with great appreciation the underwriting support of Grover Printing, a Consolidated Graphics Company.

### HISTORY, ALUMNI PROFILES AND ANECDOTES WRITER

Nora Seton, a graduate of Harvard University and Texas A&M University, is the author of three non-fiction books. She lives in Houston, where she reviews books for the *Houston Chronicle* and works as a speechwriter.

### FACULTY PROFILES WRITER

Susan Hillebrandt Santangelo ('55)

### BOOK DESIGN

HILL, Houston, Texas; Senior Designer Bobby Van Lenten

# Contents

# One Hundred Years

Now is the perfect moment to pause, to reflect and to celebrate a century of Kinkaid. What began with seven elementary school students in Margaret Kinkaid's dining room has become a vibrant campus on 40 wooded acres serving more than 1,300 students in grades prekindergarten through 12. How did this happen? Who made it happen?

The answers, at least in part, may be found in this book. The Kinkaid School has become a nationally renowned institution because of the vision of its founder and the willingness of successive headmasters to define, expand and enrich that vision. Kinkaid has never been about beautiful buildings or even state-of-the-art facilities: it has always been about people – students, faculty and staff.

This book highlights just a few of the many generations of students who have attended the School, and it recalls some of the faculty and staff who have served the School for more than 20 years. These few people represent the many Kinkaidians who have, for more than a century now, made their school and the world around it a better and more interesting place in which to live.

In 2003, the Kinkaid Centennial Celebration Steering Committee asked a small group of parents, alumni and staff to oversee the research and preparation of a special publication to honor the School's 100th anniversary. Volunteers were identified to represent each decade of the School's existence and to help gather profiles and photographs. Parents, alumni, faculty and staff, past and present, were asked to nominate alumni who might be profiled in the book. The overwhelming response was indicative both of the outstanding accomplishments of our alumni and of the enthusiasm for the project.

Since only a small, representative number could be chosen for publication in this book, the profiles were selected with specific criteria in mind. "Alumni" would include those who had attended as well as those who had graduated from Kinkaid with no specific length of time at the School being required. The alumni must have excelled in their chosen calling and in life; must have taken an interesting or unusual path in life; and must have had a positive impact on the world because of their education, values and abilities.

The faculty and staff profiled in the book also had to meet certain criteria. They must have worked at Kinkaid for 20 years or more and demonstrated a commitment to the programs and goals of the School. They also must have exemplified Kinkaid's core values of respect, responsibility, honesty and kindness and, therefore, been positive role models for our students. Additionally, they must have made a special and unique contribution to the total life of the School. ∎

**CENTENNIAL BOOK COMMITTEE CO-CHAIRS**

Roni Obermayer Atnipp
Elizabeth Jacobs Labanowski ('73)
Susan Hillebrandt Santangelo ('55)
Susan Savage Thompson

# The Margaret Kinkaid Years 1904 to 1950

Around the turn of the 20th century, Houston, a land of prairie grasses and open spaces, underwent its own industrial revolution. Timber and cotton were shipped from its port. There were 26 miles of paved streets and over 2,000 telephone customers. Trade unions engaged in successful strikes. The drilling of Spindletop (1901) and the birth of the oil industry led to extensive industrial growth. The hurricane of the century devastated Galveston, killing more than 5,000 people and sending many of the survivors north to Houston. Thomas Edison traveled to see the destruction and capture the images on his new newsreel device.

In the year 1904, Teddy Roosevelt added South and Central America to the Monroe Doctrine, and New York City opened its first subway section, from City Hall to 145th Street. In downtown Houston, a grand library was built. And Margaret Kinkaid opened a neighborhood school in her home, a small cottage on the corner of Elgin and San Jacinto Streets.

These were adventuresome times. It was not uncommon to find entrepreneurial women in Houston. Many started neighborhood schools to accommodate the burgeoning number of young children. In those days, married women were not allowed to work in the public schools, so there was a plentiful supply of married teachers from which to draw. The luckiest of Houston's children walked across the wooden plank streets or tethered their horses at Margaret Kinkaid's back steps.

Margaret Bell Culbertson Hunter was born in Houston on April 29, 1874. As a young woman, she attended the Clopper Institute of Houston, where students were given a radically modern understanding of child development. In the late 19th century, children were regarded as largely irrelevant constituents of society. They were marginalized or romanticized until they reached the age of economic productivity. But Margaret Hunter, sparked by her progressive teachers at the Clopper Institute, became committed to the observation and education of what she called "the wholly healthy child."

On Christmas Day of 1899, Margaret married William J. Kinkaid in a double-ring ceremony with her sister, Jennie Hunter. Two years later their son Hunter was born. But her passion for domesticity was no match for her passion in the classroom, and, in 1904, she started teaching in her own dining room. She recessed the School for one year, 1905, to care for her newborn second son, William. In 1906, she reopened her school and devoted herself to it for the next 46 years.

From its inception, The Kinkaid School raced to keep up with a rapidly increasing student body. Margaret Kinkaid's reputation for excellence in childhood education and personal development meant that parents well outside of the neighborhood sought her out. "My school is not a preparation for a student's life; it is his life. Mothers always want the best for their children, but it takes a good teacher to bring out the best in those children." Demand for her expertise took on its own momentum.

After two years, it was clear that a second teacher was needed. Margaret Kinkaid hired Mrs. Ballinger, an experienced elementary school teacher who had likewise married herself out of a job with the public schools. "A good teacher is made of 40% curiosity and 60% patience," Mrs. Kinkaid said. Mrs. Ballinger, like Margaret Kinkaid, believed young children needed plenty of activity in order to prepare their minds for learning. At times during the day, one could see the entire school jogging around Mrs. Kinkaid's cottage behind the multiple petticoats of young Mrs. Ballinger!

In September of 1910, the School opened to find many new families on the front steps. A line formed in front of the Elgin Street cottage. Mrs. Kinkaid's exceptional reputation had stretched down Westheimer and across the bayou to families city-wide. She borrowed $2,500 from the National Bank of Houston to add a second story to her cottage. The loan officer readily agreed; his children were enrolled at Mrs. Kinkaid's school. The plan was to hold classes downstairs, while the family lived upstairs, above the clouds of chalk dust. However, the School outgrew that space, too, and by 1917 there were six grades. The Kinkaid family had to move to make more room. Margaret Kinkaid moved her family to a house at 1401 Alabama and lived there for many years.

America's entry into World War I became official in 1917. Mrs. Kinkaid's students raised money for those suffering in Europe; others mended clothing and knitted woolens for U.S. soldiers. A current events group met weekly at the School, and Mrs. Kinkaid invited soldiers to the School to recount their experiences in this "war to end all wars."

By 1920 The Kinkaid School had 125 students. There were now eight full-time teachers. First and second graders paid $90 per year tuition, and sixth graders $130. Piano, French and Spanish were $5 to $10 extra. Margaret Kinkaid advanced the "club system," whereby students were encouraged to pursue their interests in after-school organizations. She formed the Boys' Club as an athletic venture. Eleven boys played football, coached by one of their fathers. There were community service clubs and arts clubs that developed passions in students. Margaret Kinkaid insisted that fine arts appreciation went hand-in-hand with core learning; without the two, an individual was not complete.

By 1924 The Kinkaid School reached the bursting point. R. L. Blaffer assisted Margaret Kinkaid in appointing the first Board of Trustees. It was a small but distinguished group of Houston's leading citizens: Burke Baker, R. L. Blaffer, W. L. Clayton, E. L. Neville and H. C. Wiess. This Board, along with a cadre of tenacious mothers, sold bonds for a new facility to be located on the corner of Richmond Avenue and Graustark Street in the Montrose area.

The Richmond Avenue campus opened that fall of 1924. To celebrate the opening of the new facility, Mrs. Kinkaid held a reception, a "birthday party," which started the tradition of the annual Margaret Hunter Kinkaid Open House. That year also marked the publishing of Kinkaid's school newspaper, the *Almanac*. The first issue was hectographed on one long sheet of paper by the father of student Jane Bradley. It was a school sensation.

The Richmond Avenue campus continued to grow and evolve. By 1927 there was a junior high department, and in 1938, the very first class of Kinkaid senior students matriculated. Mrs. Kinkaid's son William was appointed principal of the high school. By this time a school song, school colors and the traditions of public service and scholarships were fully established. Kinkaid boys played basketball and football under the direction of Quinn Connelly and Larry Hamilton. Miss Greenlaw oversaw the Kinkaid girls, who played basketball and volleyball. Many of the students enjoyed horseback riding in Memorial Park.

The prospect of another war in Europe cast a pall over Houston. Kinkaid's 1941 Open House included prayers for peace and a pageant of American flags. Mrs. Kinkaid emphasized to her pupils the challenges of leadership and the nobility of service to community and country. She encouraged students to sell war bonds, to collect clothing and scrap metal, and to participate in the war effort. "Concern for others," said Mrs. Kinkaid, "grows in service to others."

Gasoline shortages during World War II caused difficulty for many parents accustomed to driving their children to school. One enterprising mother arranged for the Houston city bus service to collect the children each morning after the business rush hour. Mrs. Kinkaid adjusted to this plan by opening the School slightly later than usual.

tance. "I will serve in any capacity in the School," she declared. "If the janitor was ill and the front walk needed sweeping, I'd sweep it." She was known to balk at no task – from planting flowers on the school grounds to holding a child's pet snake. When the 1950 academic year began, Mrs. Kinkaid was 76 years old, and she decided it was time to retire. The Board of Trustees reluctantly accepted her resignation, and the search began for a new leader.

Mrs. Kinkaid said, "I'm not sure a Headmistress is what we need now. A Headmaster, perhaps. A man, like William in every way, except that he should not be addicted to Coca-Colas or farming." Margaret Kinkaid herself interviewed scores of candidates, but on the day she saw John Cooper striding up the front walk, she pronounced, "That's the person I want to take over the School."

Unfortunately, Margaret Kinkaid did not enjoy many years of peaceful retirement. In 1951 she was killed in a one-car accident in Houston on her way to visit William's farm in Montgomery County. Tributes poured in at her funeral honoring one of the country's foremost visionaries in the field of education. ■

Notwithstanding grave losses to the spirit, Kinkaid flourished during the war years. The School was overcrowded with an enrollment of nearly 300 students. Mrs. Kinkaid moved to a system of double sessions to accommodate them all. Once again, Kinkaid had run out of space. This time a new Board of Trustees, led by James A. Baker, Jr., raised $100,000 for a new high school wing.

To the very end of her tenure, Margaret Kinkaid believed that any need the School might have deserved her assis-

PAGE 6: PORTRAIT OF MRS. KINKAID PAINTED BY ROBERT JOY, COMMISSIONED BY THE CLASS OF 1946; OPPOSITE TOP: MARGARET KINKAID, AGE 18; OPPOSITE LEFT: MARGARET KINKAID AND SON WILLIAM, 1916; THIS PAGE: MARGARET KINKAID AND HER HUSBAND, WILLIAM, ON VACATION, 1920

# The John Cooper Years 1951 to 1978

John Cooper, a graduate of Yale University, was rooted in the "academic East." Until his appointment at Kinkaid, he had been Headmaster of the Keith Country Day School in Rockford, Illinois. His wife, Dorothy, was a Vassar graduate with a fine mind and years of experience as a teacher. The couple moved into a house on Castle Court, adjacent to the Richmond Avenue campus. Dorothy was a patron of Kinkaid in her own right and became Kinkaid's Latin teacher when her youngest child entered school.

John Cooper's philosophy as Headmaster was succinct and eloquent. "I think that an education which develops the best in the student, which seeks to give him a sense of style, which is founded upon a belief in the love of God and the basic order of the universe, will be in harmony with and will provide vigorous support for the best in America."

As Headmaster and a member of the Houston community, John Cooper saw only opportunity where obstacles stood. When he discovered that there were no Congregational Churches in Houston, he joined with a handful of other Congregationalists to establish one. When he found that no organizations existed to satisfy his passion for light opera and Gilbert and Sullivan operettas, he created the Gilbert and Sullivan Society. He was a force behind the Kinkaid-HISD (Houston Independent School District) Engineering Math Science Summer Institute, the Burke Baker Planetarium, the First Congregational Church of Houston, the Congregational Church of The Woodlands and, much later on, The John Cooper School.

Likewise at Kinkaid, John Cooper went to work expanding and creating new programs. He organized a Dads' Club and expanded athletics – a move which greatly improved Kinkaid's reputation among high school age boys. During the 1951-1952 school year, he established a Gilbert and Sullivan tradition at the School and an annual Book Fair. He created accelerated academic programs for ambitious students and remedial summer programs for those wanting help. In order to broaden the student body, he won Board approval for a scholarship program and advanced an effort to admit children with diverse backgrounds.

But Kinkaid was bursting at the seams once again. In 1953 enrollment reached 694 students. Both John Cooper and the Board realized that nothing short of a wholesale move would accommodate the needs of the School. Originally, a 26-acre site on Alief Road was designated for the next Kinkaid campus. Hardly two years later, the City of Houston approved a plan for a major highway (the Southwest Freeway) which would cut right through the Alief site, and plans for a campus there had to be scrapped.

In 1955 a splendid and pristine tract of woodland called the "Crosswell" site in the Memorial area was proposed. This area was completely undeveloped – virtually no paved roads, no stores, no neighborhoods – just farms and forest. John Cooper led negotiations with the City of Piney Point, in which this parcel of land lay. Kinkaid was given permission to build on a 40-acre tract, and, to be a good neighbor, Kinkaid agreed to contribute $1,000 annually toward police and fire protection.

The new Memorial campus of Kinkaid was dedicated in 1957 with John Cooper presiding. The Lillie Cullen Kindergarten, the Robert Lee Blaffer Auditorium and the Walter L. Goldston Hall (the high school wing) honored those persons so instrumental in the development of the School. Several buildings were still under design. The cafeteria and arts buildings, the Moran Library, a second gymnasium, the Middle School science building and the student center were projects for the future.

John Cooper became the voice of Kinkaid. His words echoed in the school corridors. "Don't be part of the problem. Be part of the solution." A new energy spread across the campus, reflecting John Cooper's own celebrated spark and fire. Students were staying longer hours, participating in sports and theatre when classes were over. Some parents became worried at the amount of time their children remained at the School, but John Cooper assured them that the busiest students were the best students.

The excellence of Kinkaid's drama program was bolstered by the hiring of Tom and G'Ann Boyd, a husband and wife duo remembered as the "Boyd theatre legends." John Cooper added several faculty members who remained at Kinkaid throughout long and illustrious careers. Memorable teachers encouraged legions of Kinkaid students to dream tall dreams and achieve them. J. Barry Moss, an inspirational English teacher, was hailed as one of the finest debate coaches in America. Events in the early 1960's gave his teams plenty to debate: the Civil Rights marches, the Bay of Pigs invasion, the Cuban Missile Crisis and the assassination of John F. Kennedy, among other matters.

Civil defense, school security and science for survival became issues at Kinkaid and throughout the country. In 1964 the Gulf of Tonkin incident escalated tensions between the U.S. and Vietnam and led to a pledge of massive troop involvement. Mr. and Mrs. Isaac Arnold donated $150,000 toward the building of a "science and survival" facility. The Beatles made their first televised appearance on the *Ed Sullivan Show*.

The gap between young and old seemed wide and filled with tensions. Kinkaid students were "turned off" by traditional clubs and activities and opted to "do their own thing."

For Kinkaid students, the wise counsel of John Cooper was unwavering throughout. In a memorable speech to the student body, he said, "And what of your choice of friends? Of amusements? Of books? Of moral standards? In all of these we hope that you will avoid the shoddy and the inferior and that, by your choices, you will evidence a respect for what is first-rate and worthy of your best."

At the end of the 1978-1979 academic year, John Cooper resigned as Headmaster of Kinkaid after a term of 28 years. He had accomplished his goals. John Cooper's egalitarian outlook had broadened Kinkaid with diverse enrollment, financial aid and an innovative curriculum. An endowment fund had been established. The school Band Department and Interim Term had rooted and prospered. The Kinkaid School took its place among the most prestigious independent schools in the nation.

After leaving Kinkaid, John Cooper retired to The Woodlands, a community just north of Houston, to relax and slow down. But it was not long before a group of parents there persuaded him to lend his name and talents to the establishment of a private school. It was aptly named The John Cooper School, and it now competes with Kinkaid in the Southwest Preparatory Conference. John Cooper passed away at the age of 82 in April 1993. ■

**PORTRAIT OF JOHN COOPER PAINTED BY JAMES WILLS IN 1978**

# The Glenn Ballard Years 1979 to 1996

After an extensive search by the Kinkaid Board of Trustees, Glenn Ballard was persuaded to leave his position as Headmaster of The Hockaday School in Dallas to become the third Headmaster of Kinkaid. He was the unanimous choice of the Board who appreciated his youthful vigor and broad experience.

Glenn Ballard hit the ground running during the summer of 1979, before school opened. He clipped and pruned shrubs beside Julius, the groundskeeper and landscaper. He organized an army of faculty and students for the washing and whitewashing of virtually the whole School. "Ballard is a 'new broom' indeed!" claimed an observer. He was to be seen in all corners of the campus making sure that everything was shipshape.

Under Glenn Ballard's supervision, many promising programs at Kinkaid flourished. Balloon Day, the Visiting Authors Series, football festivities and Interim Term all expanded in the very first year of his administration. Administrative records were structured. An alumni magazine was initiated. The nascent Mothers' Club was advanced. Key new faculty members were attracted. Glenn Ballard immediately developed new sources for annual giving, which allowed the School to increase the number of master teachers. Eventually, he instituted a program of continuing education for the faculty as well.

Construction of the Middle School, with its beautiful Kayem Library, was one of his most rewarding projects. It solved an overcrowding issue and gave both middle and high school students a secure feeling of "place." He once said, "A sense of place is important, very important, and so excellent facilities are a must. But most important in a superior school is that yeasty mix of fine and talented faculty that makes things happen."

The far-reaching improvements were expensive. During the Glenn Ballard years, Kinkaid's endowment grew from $5 million to $50 million. His aspirations for the School seemed limitless. He was determined to make Kinkaid one of the finest private schools in the country, and he opened Kinkaid to some of the most dynamic minds of our time. He nurtured the program of Damon Wells Fellows and Weiner Fellows, bringing remarkable luminaries to speak intimately with students. Among those leaders that visited Kinkaid were James Michener, Barbara Jordan, Irving Stone, Frank Vandiver and Mortimer Adler.

Under Mr. Ballard's tenure, an Honor Code was instituted. The athletics department swelled to offer 21 sports teams for girls and boys. The theatre program expanded and an orchestra was formed. Dance became an integral piece of the arts curriculum, and photography was included. At the

same time, he believed in a core academic program. He resisted the excessively lax, "alternative" cherry-picking curriculum so much in fashion.

He prided himself on recognizing the diverse talents of the School's staff and students. He commented, "Different kinds of excellence in faculty build different kinds of excellence in students. Diversity is important. This place does not turn out a typical Kinkaid graduate. What is typical is that the students tend to be risk-takers; they tend to be very ambitious; they tend to be very self-confident. Those are the characteristics that the School produces."

Over Glenn Ballard's 17-year tenure, he rarely missed a sports event, theatre production or concert. His support of the students was total. His resolve to improve every program, faculty hire and paint job became renowned. His personal, handwritten birthday notes to students and faculty are legendary, and they are still keepsakes for many. He brought to Kinkaid a warmth and feeling of welcome. And who could forget his beloved bulldog, Dolly, who was the delight of students as she followed him around the campus and took extended naps in his office? He once said, "We're known as a hand-shaking place, a cordial and civil place, and that's good."

Glenn Ballard's retirement in 1996 signaled the end of yet another era of outstanding leadership at The Kinkaid School. He moved to Austin to pursue his many pastimes, but he has remained a part of the Kinkaid family and has seen two of his grandchildren graduate from the School. ∎

OPPOSITE: GLENN BALLARD AND DOLLY VISITING WITH LOWER SCHOOL STUDENTS, 1984; THIS PAGE: GLENN BALLARD AT GRADUATION

# The Don North Years *1996 to the present*

Don North began teaching over 35 years ago at St. Mark's School of Texas in Dallas. At the time he considered it an interim occupation before he found a "serious adult job." But he fell in love with teaching and coaching and decided after a few years that education would be his career path.

Don North came to Kinkaid as Upper School Principal in 1983. He earned such a strong reputation at Kinkaid that he was invited in 1988 to become Headmaster of Durham Academy in Durham, North Carolina.

Then, in 1996, Kinkaid contacted Don North again. Glenn Ballard was retiring, and the School wanted Don to become its new Headmaster. Mr. North said at the time that Kinkaid was the only school in America that could have lured him away from Durham Academy. His wife was happily teaching at Durham Academy, and his youngest daughter was a tenth grader there. But, as he observed, "Kinkaid is a special school. What the School can offer students, parents, faculty and staff is remarkable. The opportunity to return to Kinkaid as Headmaster was impossible to resist."

Don North is a believer in strategic planning, and soon after his arrival, Kinkaid embarked on comprehensive, formal long-term planning. The planning led first to the installation of a campus-wide, fiber-optic network and enhancements in technology that put Kinkaid in the vanguard of technology use among independent day schools. It next led to the inauguration of the most ambitious fundraising campaign in the history of the School. *Building for the Next Century* raised $47 million, and resulted in the construction of three new buildings (the Friedkin Family Lower School Building, the Kinkaid Theatre and the Center for Student Life, Fine Arts and Administration), a beautiful and popular quadrangle, an attractive and distinctive clock tower and two Lower School playgrounds, and the addition of over $7 million to

the endowment. "Space that is designed and built with great care and skill communicates powerful messages to those who will work in that space, and leads inevitably to greater learning and accomplishment," he commented. The capital campaign was one of the largest among day schools in the country at the time and drew national attention to Kinkaid and to Don North's leadership.

With the campaign well under way, Don North turned his attention to internal affairs. The strategic planning that led to the capital campaign had also identified increased interest among parents in character development. The School adopted four core values – honesty, respect, responsibility and kindness – and hired a Director of Character Education. "I think of character as the collective habits that guide our lives," Don observed, "habits of the heart, habits of the mind,

habits of the spirit. Our job is to help our students develop and strengthen these habits." Up until the 2004-2005 academic year, Don North taught English in the Upper School every year. He was elected President of ISAS (Independent School Association of the Southwest) in 2005.

Looking forward, Don North is focused on making character education an integral part of the school culture and not simply another program. He is committed to preparing Kinkaid students for the increasingly global and diverse world they will enter as adults. Under his leadership the School's athletic and arts programs continue to thrive and to play a central role in the lives of many Kinkaid students. "Both the arts," North says, "and athletics serve a deeper educational pur-

pose, for they are among the best ways our School has of encouraging students to look beyond their own field of vision and to develop the courage to take healthy risks." Finally, Don North is committed to ensuring that Kinkaid maintains the highest academic excellence and quality faculty possible. "In the last few years at Kinkaid we have built several extraordinary facilities that have enriched the educational experiences of our students immeasurably. But at the core of this experience are caring, skilled, passionate teachers – teachers who make a difference in the lives of our students," Don North recently wrote. ∎

**OPPOSITE: DON NORTH IN THE BROWN AUDITORIUM; ABOVE: DON NORTH VISITING WITH LOWER SCHOOL STUDENTS IN HIS OFFICE**

## NAUGHTY BOYS

*O*n the Elgin Street campus was a huge magnolia tree, under which students picnicked with their lunches. Children either brought their lunches, or these lunches were delivered to them around noon. There was much competition among the girls as to whose lunch basket was prettier. All the boys at one time or another carved their initials into the giant magnolia trunk. Margaret Kinkaid watched with raised eyebrows. "Believe it or not," Mrs. Kinkaid once said, "I'm partial to naughty boys, for they often grow to be creative men."

## SIMPLE DRESSING

*M*rs. Kinkaid required modest behavior and dress in the classroom. "Simple dressing" was encouraged for girls even at the School on Elgin Street, but at the Richmond Avenue campus, it was insisted upon.

In 1930 Kinkaid girls took a "simple dressing pledge," which stated that they would wear no rouge, no lipstick and no unnecessary jewelry. Dresses of silk, satin and velvet were banned, as were chiffon and silk stockings. In spite of some alluring new hair styles – bobs particularly – Kinkaid girls pledged that they would not have permanent waves during the school term. For any violation of this code, a 25 cent penalty was exacted.

# Josephine Abercrombie

Josephine Abercrombie ('42) remembers fondly the "camaraderie of all the students at Kinkaid." She brought that spirit into a life of boundless initiatives.

Abercrombie's life is a collage of achievements. She has been a prize-winning horsewoman, a breeder and owner of champion racehorses, a boxing promoter and a philanthropist. She has made her home in Versailles, Kentucky, having built one of the finest examples of Palladian architecture in the country. Her home is also the setting for Pin Oak Stud.

Abercrombie's father, the late Houston oilman J. S. Abercrombie, was the founder of the annual Pin Oak Horse Show in Houston in 1945. The show became known as the Pin Oak Charity Horse Show, dedicated to raising funds for the building and continuing support of Texas Children's Hospital. Josephine Abercrombie continues the family's tradition of charitable giving as President of The Abercrombie Foundation.

Following in the footsteps of her father, Abercrombie has acted as President of Pin Oak Stud, President of J. A. Interests (real estate and oil), President of The Abercrombie Foundation and founder of The Lexington School. She also sits on the Boards of several distinguished institutions including Rice University Board of Governors, The Texas Children's Hospital, the Grayson–Jockey Club Research Foundation and The Lexington School.

To top off such wide-ranging accomplishments, Abercrombie is also the author of a children's book, *Charlie the Horse,* and the lyrics of "Lonely's Only Me," a song recorded by Kristy Lee in 2003.

## Daniel C. Arnold

Daniel C. Arnold ('47) recalls that Kinkaid gave him "a sound academic base, and lifetime friendships and social graces, which have been very instrumental in letting me achieve what I have in life." He fondly remembers playing six-man football on the Richmond Avenue campus.

Arnold received undergraduate and law degrees from the University of Texas. He practiced law with Vinson & Elkins for many years. He then served as President and later Chairman of the Board of First City Bancorporation of

Texas. Finally, he became Chairman of the Board and CEO of Farm & Home Financial Corporation. Paralleling his distinguished career was Arnold's dedication to community service. He served on the Boards of the Harris County Hospital District, Baylor College of Medicine, the American Red Cross, the Metropolitan Transit Authority and many more organizations.

"I have always been of the belief that one should seek to give more back to his or her community than one takes from it."

## James A. Baker III

James Baker III ('48) graduated from Princeton University in 1952 and served as a Lieutenant in the Marine Corps. He received a law degree with honors from the University of Texas Law School.

After practicing law for several years, Baker embarked on a career in government. He accepted senior government positions under four United States Presidents. He was Under Secretary of Commerce for President Gerald Ford. He managed tremendous post-Cold War instability as Secretary of State under President George H.W. Bush. He was White House Chief of Staff and

President Ronald Reagan and also Chairman of the President's Economic Policy Council. He served as Secretary of State, White House Chief of Staff and Senior Counselor to the President under George H.W. Bush. Most recently, Baker functioned as Special Presidential Envoy on the issue of Iraq debt for President George W. Bush.

In 1991 James Baker III received the Presidential Medal of Freedom. His other distinguished honors are too numerous to list, but include Princeton's Woodrow Wilson Award, Harvard's John F. Kennedy School of

Kennan Award, the Department of the Treasury's Alexander Hamilton Award and the Department of State's Distinguished Service Award.

Baker is currently a senior partner in the law firm of Baker Botts and honorary Chairman of the James A. Baker III Institute for Public Policy at Rice University. He serves the nation frequently in the capacity of Elder Statesman.

In 1985 and 2005, James Baker III gave the Commencement speech to Kinkaid's graduating seniors – an honor his father had performed for the School in 1939.

# Thomas D. Barrow

Thomas Barrow ('41) was a student on the Richmond Avenue campus from 1930 to 1938. He remembers Margaret Kinkaid declaring, "Stand up straight and speak out! Don't mumble! Make people listen, but be certain what you say is worthwhile."

Barrow certainly took the advice to heart. He earned multiple graduate degrees, became President of Humble Oil, Senior Vice President of Exxon Corporation and Chairman of Kennecott Copper Company. Barrow eventually retired as Vice Chairman of the Standard Oil Company of Ohio in June 1985.

In addition to his eminent professional career, Barrow's history of community service is legendary. He has served as trustee to countless organizations, including Baylor College of Medicine, Houston Grand Opera, the Texas Medical Center, the American Museum of Natural History, the New York Philharmonic Orchestra, Stanford University, Winrock International and more. He served on Kinkaid's Board of Trustees from 1970 to 1972 and the Alumni Association Board from 1994 to 1997. What Barrow has had to say, Mrs. Kinkaid would agree, has been truly worthwhile.

# Audrey Jones Beck

Audrey Jones Beck ('39) entered Kinkaid as a kindergartner in 1927. The granddaughter of Jesse H. Jones, she was interested in fine arts from childhood. Through her love of Impressionism and Post-Impressionism, she began a scholarly collection of masterpieces that now form the core holdings of the Museum of Fine Arts, Houston.

In 1942 Audrey Jones married John Beck, a financier and owner of Boehck Engineering. "I told John of my dream to collect a representative group of Impressionist works for Houston. He thought his wife had gone quite mad."

During the 1950's and 1960's, dealers from around the world visited Beck, ferrying their finest paintings to Houston in hopes of her positive reception. Her collection immediately appreciated in value, so much so that her husband left his financial career to join her. Together they made a philanthropic team passionate about the arts of Houston and memorable for their munificence.

# George Bellows

George Bellows ('42) attended Rice University. He served in the U.S. Navy during World War II. Upon returning to the United States, Bellows earned a civil engineering degree from the University of Texas. He joined his father and brothers at the W. S. Bellows Construction Corporation as an engineer, eventually becoming President from 1979 to 1986. He was responsible for building such local landmarks as the Alley Theatre, the Wortham Center, One Shell Plaza, First City Tower and the Tenneco Building (now El Paso Energy Building), Bellows's personal favorite.

Bellows was a member of the Texas Medical Center Board from 1976 until his death in May 2005. He joined the Board of Texas Children's Hospital in 1967 and served as Board President from 1973 to 1975 and as Chairman in 1983. Bellows also served on the Hospital Building Committee from 1971 until 1988 and from 1994 until his death.

In recognition of his extensive efforts in building Houston's Medical Center, a street between the Abercrombie and West Buildings was named in honor of Bellows and his wife, Ann.

And it was W. S. Bellows Construction Corporation that served as general contractor for Kinkaid's most recent building program.

# Laura Lee Scurlock Blanton

Laura Lee Scurlock Blanton ('46) was so busy at Kinkaid that "all her friends ever saw of her was a brown-haired whirl streaking past them on her way to the gym or study hall."

Scurlock attended Southern Methodist University and the University of Texas. Typical of Scurlock, her love of both universities led her to champion their causes and futures. She served as a member of the SMU Board of Trustees, raising over $30 million for their capital campaign.

Scurlock's reputation for "hands-on" philanthropy made her a hero within the Houston community. She was a lifetime member of M.D. Anderson's Board of Visitors, a program of prominent civic leaders focusing their expertise and compassion on cancer patients.

With her husband, Jack Blanton, Scurlock funded a new building for the art museum at the University of Texas and acted as Chairman of the Glassell School of Art. She later served as President of the Scurlock Foundation, giving her generous support to Houston's Museum of Fine Arts, the Houston Public Library, the Salvation Army, the Texas Medical Center and more.

# William Blattner

William Blattner, M.D. ('62), graduated from Washington University School of Medicine. He completed residencies at the New York Cornell Medical Center and Memorial Sloan-Kettering Cancer Institute. Blattner then trained as an oncologist at the National Cancer Institute in Bethesda, Maryland. He served in the Environmental Epidemiology Branch for over 20 years, retiring in 1995 as founding Chief of the Viral Epidemiology Branch.

Blattner conducted pioneering research into the epidemiology and prevention of the human retroviruses HIV and HTLV. As Director of the Institute of Human Virology's HIV Vaccine Trials Unit, Blattner works tirelessly to find a cure for HIV and to accelerate access to promising pharmaceuticals. He plays a key role in the President's Emergency Plan for AIDS Relief in underdeveloped countries, training and organizing optimal HIV therapies for afflicted populations worldwide.

On his senior yearbook page, Blattner quoted, "For man is man and the master of his fate." He has pursued that philosophy, to the benefit of all mankind.

## Lisa Brannon-Peppas

Even at Kinkaid, Lisa Brannon-Peppas ('80) knew that she wanted a Ph.D. in engineering so that she could conduct her own research to cure disease. Kinkaid, she said, gave her the belief that she could accomplish anything. She received her B.S. in chemical engineering from Rice, and her M.S. and Ph.D. in chemical engineering from Purdue.

Brannon-Peppas conducted research for Eli Lilly & Company, investigating a variety of drug delivery systems. Biodegradable polymers seemed to offer significant promise. Unwavering in her focus and resolve, Brannon-Peppas founded Biogel Technology, Inc., a research and development company focused on targeted and biodegradable systems to treat cancer and other life-threatening conditions.

Most recently, Brannon-Peppas joined the faculty of the University of Texas College of Engineering, where she continues her work as a Research Professor and Entrepreneur in Residence.

# PAINTING MRS. KINKAID

*M*y friend, Joyce Ledbetter ('46), was having her portrait painted by the artist Robert Joy. During those afternoons, I would go home from school with her, and we would chat while she posed. One afternoon Joyce and I speculated about what our senior class gift to Mrs. Kinkaid should be. We asked Robert Joy if he would consider painting a portrait of Mrs. Kinkaid. He said, "Yes, and it would cost $10,000."

My father was on the Board of Trustees, and I went to him and asked how I could obtain the money. He gave me $1,000 and told me that I would have to raise the rest. He suggested that I try the Board of Trustees first.

Our Class of 1946 was the first to publish a yearbook, and I was already visiting businessmen downtown in the afternoons to raise money for ads for the yearbook. "Tiny," a very tall and overweight policeman on horseback, used to follow me down the street and watch over me as I went from office to office. I knew where the members of the Board of Trustees worked, and I went to their offices to ask for a donation. Every trustee gave me $1,000, and so we had the money for the portrait.

At the end of Honor Day, in the gym, our senior class revealed that we were commissioning a portrait of Mrs. Kinkaid. Mrs. Kinkaid was stunned, but we knew she couldn't refuse if it was announced in front of the whole school.

Many years later I looked back on the incident and wondered if Papa had coerced the Board members to contribute the $1,000 or if he actually told them to give me a check, and he'd pay them back. I never knew.

CARO IVY WALKER, CLASS OF 1946

# THE BIRTHDAY PARTY

*I*n the summer of 1924, construction of the Richmond Avenue campus began. School started a few weeks late that autumn, and students coped with the sounds of hammers and
workmen throughout the building.

Mrs. Kinkaid proposed a reception in December to celebrate the move from Elgin Street to Richmond
Avenue. She referred to it as the Birthday Party commemorating the "birth" of the new campus.

For generations after that, many students thought the event was a celebration of Mrs. Kinkaid's
own birthday, and they referred to it as "Mrs. Kinkaid's Birthday Party." Always gracious, Mrs. Kinkaid
never corrected their mistake, and it was many years before the true story was widely known.

This event became one of Kinkaid's oldest traditions. It is now referred to as "The Margaret
Hunter Kinkaid Open House."

# George W. Bush

George W. Bush ('64) showed political promise as a young teenager at Kinkaid when he served as Vice President of the freshman class in 1961. His eighth grade history teacher Art Goddard remembered in particular his well-written and prescient paper on presidential politics. He left Kinkaid for boarding school after ninth grade and then attended Yale University.

He served as an F-102 fighter pilot in the Texas Air National Guard. He received an M.B.A. from Harvard Business School and returned to his hometown, Midland, Texas, to begin a career in the energy business. He then moved to Dallas after becoming an owner of the Texas Rangers. Bush was elected Governor of Texas in 1994 and became the first governor in Texas history to be elected to consecutive four-year terms. As Governor, George W. Bush earned a reputation for bipartisanship and compassionate leadership.

George W. Bush became the 43rd President of the United States on January 20, 2001. In 2004 he was re-elected, and although well-known for cutting taxes and comprehensive education reform, President Bush's tenure was most strikingly affected by the terrorist attacks of September 11, 2001. His invasion of Afghanistan and subsequent war against Iraq compelled the international community to recognize terrorism as a material threat to our world. He has pledged to make the world a more secure place for all people. President Bush trusts that the future of our world depends on the building of free and prosperous societies.

## John Ellis "Jeb" Bush

John Ellis "Jeb" Bush ('70) attended Kinkaid from fifth grade through ninth grade. In 1998, he was elected Florida's 43rd Governor, and in 2002 he became the first Republican to be re-elected in the state's history.

During his two terms, Governor Bush has revolutionized the education system to achieve dramatic student achievement, and provided broad-based tax relief and economic incen-

tives to strengthen and diversify Florida's economy.

Governor Bush's "A+ Plan for Education," established in 1999, raised standards and increased accountability and funding for Florida's public schools. In 2005, 71% of fourth graders are reading at or above grade level, compared to only 48% in 1999. In addition to his improvements in education, Floridians have received $14 billion in

tax relief as well as leading the nation in job growth since 2002. Florida is the top tourist destination in the world.

Prior to being elected Governor, Bush was a principal in running one of the largest, full-service commercial real estate companies in South Florida. In 1987-1988, Governor Bush served as Florida's Secretary of Commerce, promoting the state's excellent business environment worldwide.

# A. J. Carothers

Writing success came early to A. J. Carothers ('50), who wrote his first story, a murder mystery, at age nine and sold it to a classmate for fifteen cents.

After attending Northwestern University and UCLA, Carothers combined his dramatic instincts with his literary flair to write screenplays. After several years under contract to CBS and then Walt Disney, he became a freelance writer, scripting TV series, TV movies and feature films for various studios and networks. No doubt thousands of Kinkaidians have heard the resonant dialogues of A. J. Carothers's characters on screens large and small. For some years now, Carothers has returned to Kinkaid to teach one of the most popular courses offered during Interim Term.

# Gibson Carothers

Gibson Carothers ('62), labeled by Kinkaid English teacher Ann Clifford as a "goofy cutup," attended Southern Methodist University and graduated from the University of California, Berkeley. He began his professional career as an advertising *wunderkind*. However, at the age of only 30, he felt he had already exhausted the possibilities within advertising. Carothers took a chance when some friends suggested he contribute ideas to a greeting card company they were starting. He never looked back.

When his jokes don't show up on television, they often appear on products. Carothers coined such famous phrases as: "I love my job, it's the work I hate," and "Life's a beach." He conceived of a wastebasket with the words "Thanks for your suggestions" written on its side. Next came a dog dish with "This tastes like dog food" and an alarm clock with "Wake up! You can sleep at work!"

Carothers continues to make the world giggle. He strives relentlessly to write the next funniest joke.

# Charlie Carson

Charlie Carson ('65) credits Kinkaid with "preparing me to become an engineer and a team player." After receiving a degree in electrical engineering from Texas A&M University, Carson was impelled by his profound Christian faith to find ways of helping people in need.

Perhaps Carson's most enduring legacy is his ministry on the Board of Directors of Living Water International. Unsafe water is responsible for the spread of disease and death among most of the world's impoverished cultures. More than two billion people on earth are without basic sanitation. Living Water International is committed to bringing clean, uncontaminated water to indigent and underdeveloped cultures around the world. The organization uses both portable and truck-mounted rigs for drilling deep water wells where only polluted surface sources existed before. As people gather to witness the goings-on, Living Water International team members have the opportunity to conduct Bible schools, medical clinics and hygiene clinics, and to share the Gospel.

# John B. Cassidy

John B. Cassidy ('68) still remembers his teachers at Kinkaid. "I could name them all today. They taught with passion and commitment. I think especially of Mrs. Ann T. Clifford, my English teacher, who had a contagious love for life and literature."

Cassidy received a B.A. and M.A. Ed. from Stanford University. In 1978, fueled by the unlikely success of a book on how to juggle, he and two college mates founded Klutz, Inc., a children's book publishing company in Palo Alto, California. Twenty-five years and 124 titles later, the three sold it to Scholastic, Inc., which continues to publish the books around the world today under the Klutz imprint.

# Mary Frances Bowles Couper

Mary Frances Bowles Couper ('28) studied directly under Margaret Kinkaid. She attended the University of Texas and later endowed two Presidential Scholarships for undergraduate students in piano performance.

Couper was a founder of the Kappa Alpha Theta Charity Antiques Show, one of the premier antiques shows in the nation. In addition, she was a sponsor of Bayou Bend Collection and Gardens and the Memorial Hermann Hospital System. Known for her extreme humility and generosity, Couper was devoted to the Junior League of Houston and its wide-reaching community services. Her charitable accomplishments have helped thousands of Houstonians.

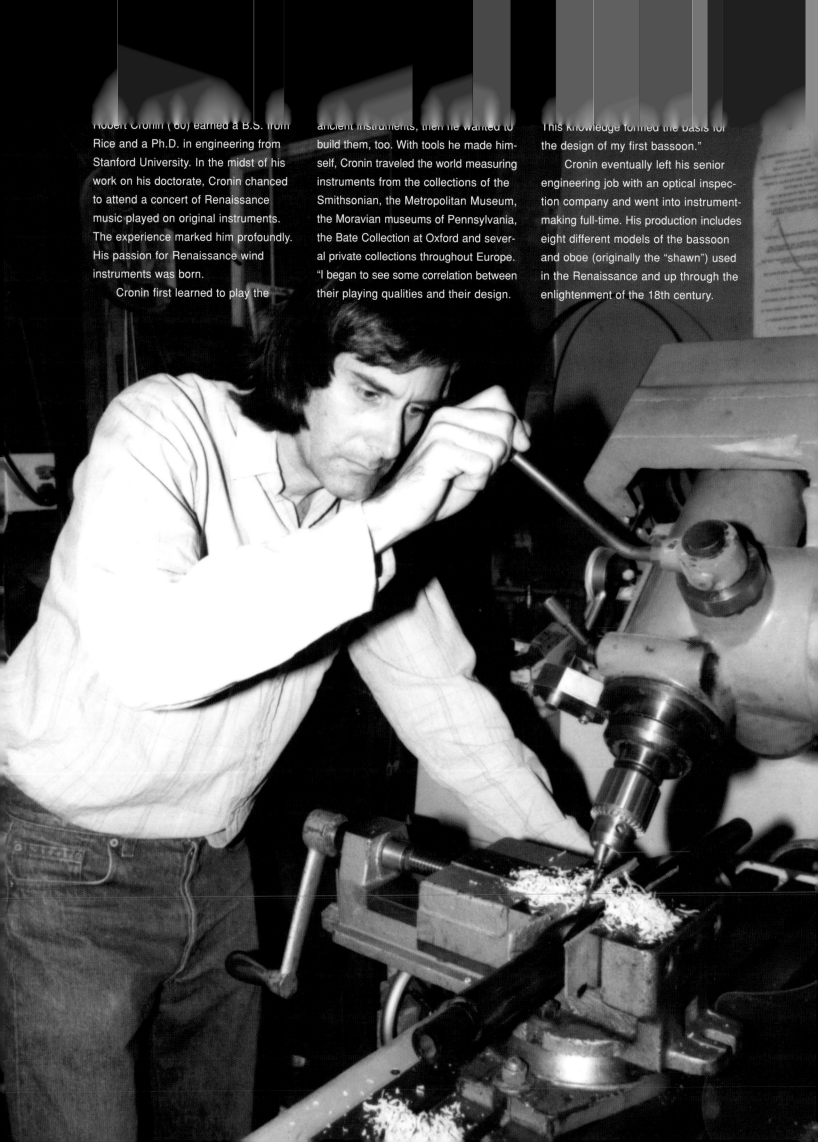

Robert Cronin ( '60) earned a B.S. from Rice and a Ph.D. in engineering from Stanford University. In the midst of his work on his doctorate, Cronin chanced to attend a concert of Renaissance music played on original instruments. The experience marked him profoundly. His passion for Renaissance wind instruments was born.

Cronin first learned to play the ancient instruments, then he wanted to build them, too. With tools he made himself, Cronin traveled the world measuring instruments from the collections of the Smithsonian, the Metropolitan Museum, the Moravian museums of Pennsylvania, the Bate Collection at Oxford and several private collections throughout Europe. "I began to see some correlation between their playing qualities and their design.

This knowledge formed the basis for the design of my first bassoon."

Cronin eventually left his senior engineering job with an optical inspection company and went into instrument-making full-time. His production includes eight different models of the bassoon and oboe (originally the "shawn") used in the Renaissance and up through the enlightenment of the 18th century.

# Emily and Holcombe Crosswell

Emily Attwell Crosswell ('59) and Holcombe Crosswell ('58) launched themselves from Kinkaid for a lifetime of community service. Both attended the University of Texas.

Holcombe Crosswell took part in the family investment business and is currently President of Griggs Corporation. His involvement in community service is lengendary. He has acted as Chairman of the Board of Trustees of Texas Children's Hospital, Vice Chairman of the Texas Medical Center, Chairman of the Board of Directors of the Metropolitan Transit Authority and as a member of the Board of Directors of Centerpoint Energy. At Kinkaid he has served as trustee, Board member, Board Chairman and trustee of the Kinkaid Investments Foundation.

Emily Crosswell says, "I experienced leadership opportunities at Kinkaid, and relished the atmosphere that taught us that one can achieve whatever one wishes."

She has served on the Board of several Texas Children's Hospital initiatives, as a member of the Board of Trustees of The Methodist Hospital System and as a founder of the Houston Police Foundation. In addition, Crosswell has brought her leadership to the Board of Directors of the Museum of Natural Science, the Ronald McDonald House and the Greater Houston Community Foundation. She has also served on the Boards of the Junior League of Houston, the DePelchin Children's Center, the Greater Houston Convention and Visitors Bureau, and the Women's Resource Center of Greater Houston, among many others.

Holcombe reflects that he was "raised in a family which was dedicated to giving back to the community." Together, he and Emily have embellished that fine legacy.

# Charles Dillingham

Charles Dillingham ('61) made the most of his senior year at Kinkaid – he was the co-editor of *The Falcon,* President of the Student Council and the lead in the school play *Cyrano.* He went on to receive his B.A. in English at Yale and stayed on to complete an M.F.A. in theatre administration from Yale's celebrated Drama School. Straightaway he was hired as General Manager of the American Conservatory Theatre in San Francisco.

He is currently the Managing Director of Center Theatre Group in Los Angeles where he supervises all development, marketing, administrative and financial aspects of the Abmanson Theater and the Mark Taper Forum.

Prior to joining Center Theatre Group, he was President and CEO of an international production and management company in New York, which presented the Bolshoi Ballet and Opera, the Kirov Ballet and Opera, and the Royal Ballet at the Metropolitan Opera House and on national tour.

He was the General Manager and then Executive Director of the American Ballet Theatre for eight years, during which time the world-renowned company toured Paris and Japan, made 10 television productions and mounted 75 new productions. He has also served as the Managing Director of the Brooklyn Academy of Music Theatre Company.

Dillingham has also served as Chairman of the Board of Dance / USA, on the Board of Directors of Theatre L.A. and on theatre advisory panels at the California Arts Council and the National Endowment for the Arts.

# Adam Ereli

Adam Ereli ('79) earned a B.A. from Yale and an M.A. in international relations from the Fletcher School of Law and Diplomacy. Fluent in French and Arabic, he worked as a journalist and human rights activist in Paris.

Ereli joined the Foreign Service in 1989 and served in Egypt, Syria, Ethiopia and Yemen. Upon returning to Washington, D.C., he accepted the position of Director of the Office of Press and Public Affairs in the Bureau of Near Eastern Affairs, and later acted as Director of the Office of Press Relations in the Bureau of Public Affairs.

After serving as Deputy Chief of Mission at the U.S. Embassy in Qatar, Ereli became Deputy Spokesman of the Department of State in 2003.

In speaking to Kinkaid's Upper School student body, Ereli stressed that "a character formed of humility and empathy would be the strongest during times of adversity."

# Clark Kent Ervin

After graduating from Kinkaid, Clark Ervin ('77) earned a B.A. from Harvard, an M.A. from Oxford University as a Rhodes Scholar and a law degree from Harvard Law School. He remembers the teachers and administrators at Kinkaid who propelled him to a career in public service.

"I am grateful to John Cooper for having enough faith in my ability to admit me to Kinkaid as well as grateful to Art Goddard, from whom I learned the beauty and majesty of history, and J. Barry Moss and Brent Northup, who taught me how to debate, speak and write persuasively."

Ervin served in both Bush administrations and was Assistant Secretary of State in Texas during President George W. Bush's tenure as Governor. He became the first Inspector General of the Department of Homeland Security in 2003. In January 2005, Ervin became the Paul H. Nitze Fellow at the Aspen Institute and Director of its newly established Homeland Security Initiative at the Aspen Institute.

"I look forward to developing what I hope will be the nation's premier opportunity for policymakers, scholars and industry to exchange information and ideas in this vitally important issue area, and to consider, debate and propose solutions to homeland security problems."

# Marie Fay Evnochides

Marie Fay Evnochides ('59) wrote: "Mr. Cooper was my lifelong mentor from the first day I came to Kinkaid until he retired in 1979." Evnochides went on to Sarah Lawrence College where an introductory early childhood education course completely captured her imagination and zeal.

Evnochides was hired by John Cooper in 1965 to establish and teach a program for three-year-olds. She became Director of Kinkaid's Pre-School in 1973. After 25 wonderful teaching years, Evnochides left in 1990 to become the founder of a new school on the grounds of her childhood home in Houston. The Fay School is a co-educational, not-for-profit, non-sectarian school, which educates children ages 3-11 in a highly challenging, yet loving and nurturing environment. The Fay School is a testament to Evnochides's love of teaching and philosophy of lifelong learning.

# David Louis Finegold

David Louis Finegold ('81) graduated summa cum laude from Harvard University and, as a Rhodes Scholar, earned a Ph.D. in political science from Oxford University. David credits his experience fielding tough questions while a debater under the tutelage of Jim Fleissner as a key reason for his success in the Rhodes process.

Finegold's research initially focused on the design of effective organizations and comparing education and training systems among industrialized countries. Reform of training strategies and maximization of worker skills and productivity have formed the core of his inquiry. Finegold has also consulted on the changing employer / employee relationship in a highly technical world. More recently, his work has focused on strategic, organizational and ethical issues in the biotech industry. He has co-authored a number of books on corporate governance and bioindustry ethics.

Currently, Finegold serves as Professor of Strategy & Organization Studies at the Keck Graduate Institute of Applied Life Sciences in Claremont, California.

# Walter W. Fondren III

Walter W. Fondren III ('54) achieved
great fame in Texas athletics. He
remembers Kinkaid Coach Jarvis
Watson convinced him he could be
"competitive at a higher level." Truer
words were never spoken. Fondren
went on to become a highly honored
Longhorn football star, and after graduating from the University of Texas with
a degree in geology, he was drafted
into the NFL by the Los Angeles Rams,
although he never chose to play on the
professional level.

Fondren, also an avid sportsman,
was a founder of the Texas Coastal
Conservation Association. This organization grew from a handful of concerned
fishermen to a nationally recognized
coastal management organization with
over 90,000 members throughout the
Gulf Coast and up the Atlantic seaboard.
Fondren is currently its Chairman of the
Board. He has won innumerable awards
for his leadership and dedication to
marine resource management.

# Cullen Geiselman, Wilhelmina Cullen Smith and Beth Robertson

For Cullen Geiselman ('93), "Kinkaid's Interim Term exposed me to the world's environmental problems in a Gulf Coast crisis class." Geiselman inherited an interest in bats from her mother, and Kinkaid, she declares, "taught me how to advocate for myself and build a life around my own somewhat bizarre interests." Directly upon graduating from Kinkaid, Geiselman pioneered the first-ever internship at the Houston Zoo, assisting keepers in the Primate Center.

She attended Duke University, and then spent years working for Bat Conservation International in Austin, Texas, developing educational programs and advancing in-depth research on bat habits and environmental relevance. She is already con-

sidered an expert in her field and is affectionately known by many as "the bat lady." Currently, she is earning her Ph.D. at Columbia University in the Ecology, Evolution, and Environmental Biology Department.

Geiselman's mother, Beth Robertson ('64) received a degree in classics from the University of Texas and immediately turned her life toward philanthropy. She has served as Chair of the Board of Regents of the University of Houston, trustee of the Museum of Fine Arts, Houston, Head of the Roundtable at the Baker Institute, Chair of the Board of The Cullen Trust for Health Care and trustee of The Cullen Foundation, among other civic offices. She has even acted as Board

member and Chair of Bat Conservation International, supporting the passion of her daughter, Cullen Geiselman.

Geiselman's grandmother, Wilhelmina Cullen Robertson Smith ('40) likewise became a pillar of the Houston community. She has generously supported the arts, education and medical care. Glenn Ballard described Wilhelmina Smith as "a legendary member of a legendary family." Her tireless work as Head of The Cullen Foundation has had a direct and munificent impact on Kinkaid. The Cullen Foundation has funded chairs in mathematics and science, and supported the Kinkaid-HISD Engineering Math Science Summer Institute for minority students for over 20 years.

## PURPLE AND GOLD

*In 1918 11 Kinkaid boys, under the tutelage of one boy's father, formed a football club. Because they numbered so few, they played both offense and defense. When the team needed uniforms to compete against other school clubs, Joe Hudson's father suggested the colors orange and blue, those of his alma mater, the University of Virginia; but the Kinkaid girls roundly objected to this color combination. Purple and gold were selected after debate and compromise. Mrs. Kinkaid was not enthusiastic, but she abided by the students' decision. Nonetheless, for many years the boys played football in khaki pants and blue shirts because gold and purple shirts were hard to find, and no one even considered ordering uniforms for a handful of boys.*

## KINKAID, MY OWN KINKAID

*Charlotte Williams Darby remembers a slumber party at Elizabeth Law's house in 1921. The girls, both in sixth grade, sat at the dining room table dreaming up ways to promote school spirit. In that one night they wrote a school song sung to the tune of "Maryland, My Maryland." Mrs. Kinkaid was delighted. "Kinkaid, My Own Kinkaid," slightly revised, continues to be sung today.*

## THE FALCON

*An exuberant "Purple and Gold Mania" hit Kinkaid each football season in the late 1940's. Boys playing on the six-man team worked out clever tricks for scoring. Jim Glass, one of the football stars, made yet another contribution to Kinkaid in 1946. Mrs. Kinkaid chose his design of a falcon as the official school symbol. For many years Jim's design was used on decals and sports letter jackets. Today, the Kinkaid falcon is a familiar sight throughout Houston.*

## THE DOUGHNUT TALE

*C*ivics class was offered in the second semester of our senior year. It was taught by Mr. William Kinkaid himself – "Willie," we affectionately called him to his back.

Mr. Kinkaid was calm, low-key, laid-back and fun. Our class was at 10 o'clock, the time of modern day coffee breaks. Our classroom was in the front room of the senior wing. The building was U-shaped, and so we had a perfect view of things – we could see if Mrs. Kinkaid was making one of her checks on the School. We had a safety watch.

Weingarten Grocery was directly across from the School on Richmond Avenue at Graustark Street. Once a week we opened the tall, floor-to-ceiling window and sent a chosen messenger for doughnuts – all of this with Mr. Kinkaid's blessing. Somehow, the best Civics classes were on doughnut days. And to our knowledge, Mrs. Kinkaid never knew!

JANE HOFFERT MOORE, CLASS OF 1946

# Scott Heumann

Scott Heumann ('69) took all the poetry and prose awards that he won during his years at Kinkaid and sailed into a career of literary distinction. What a blessing that he landed again in Houston, bringing his fine ear and indefatigable spirit to the Houston Grand Opera. First as dramaturge, and later as Assistant Director, Heumann invented the use of surtitles during an opera. Surtitles are the English translation of a libretto that opera-goers may read above the stage. Moreover, because Heumann was fluent in several European languages, he could personally confirm that the English translation was faithful, bearing the full weight of its original operatic force.

Until his death in 1993, Heumann traveled around the world searching out superior voices. Always in pursuit of quality, he was renowned for bringing many new stars to the Houston stage.

# William P. Hobby, Jr.

William P. Hobby, Jr. ('49), was a student at Kinkaid for seven years and fondly remembers the sense of community and family which Kinkaid instilled in even its youngest students. He then attended Rice University and then entered the United States Navy where he served four years in naval intelligence. Returning to Houston, Hobby joined the staff of *The Houston Post,* at that time published by his father. Promoted through the ranks, he eventually became Executive Editor and President of the paper for nearly 20 years, until the paper's sale in 1983.

At a young age Hobby became Senate Parliamentarian of the 56th Texas Legislature. President Lyndon B. Johnson appointed Hobby to the Presidential Task Force on Suburban Problems and to the National Citizens' Advisory Committee on Vocational Rehabilitation. Hobby was also named to the Texas Air Control Board.

In 1972, Hobby was elected Texas Lieutenant Governor. He presided over the Senate of the 63rd Legislature. As Chairman of the Legislative Budget Board, he streamlined fiscal and budget processes. Hobby served as Lieutenant Governor for 18 years, during which time he was a champion of Texas's public schools and higher education.

Hobby continues to hold professorships at the University of Texas, Rice University and the UT Health Science Center. He is on the Board of Regents of the University of Houston and was selected to become Chancellor of the University as well.

# Katherine Susman Howe

Katherine Susman Howe ('64) volunteered for the Junior Red Cross during her years at Kinkaid, becoming Vice President of the Harris County Junior Red Cross chapter. During her junior and senior years, she was also an active member of the debate team. Her accomplishments befit her yearbook quotation: "Thy modesty's a candle to thy merit."

Howe studied art history at Connecticut College, where she received a B.A., and earned an M.A. from the Cooperstown Graduate Program, part of the SUNY system. She was Curator of the New Haven Colony Historical Society before returning to Houston in 1971 to marry George Howe ('64). In 1975 she became Associate Curator of the Museum of Fine Arts, Houston, Bayou Bend Collection. The following year she was transferred to the main museum, where she rose through the ranks to become Curator of Decorative Arts. In 1993 she also became Director of Rienzi, the former home of Harris and Carroll Sterling Masterson ('28) and the museum's collection of European decorative arts. She has co-authored several exhibition catalogues and the Junior League of Houston's book *Houston's Forgotten Heritage* (1991). Several of the exhibitions for which she has been a curator have received grants from the National Endowment for the Arts and the National Endowment for the Humanities. Exhibitions she has organized have traveled to the Metropolitan, San Francisco, High and Minneapolis Museums of Art and the Smithsonian Institution.

"Through art I have been fortunate to learn about new and interesting worlds and to enable others to learn about them as well."

# Thaddeus Thomson Hutcheson

Thaddeus Thomson Hutcheson ('30), known to his classmates as Thad, was a student at the Richmond Avenue campus. He went on to receive top honors at Princeton University and the University of Texas School of Law, and promptly joined the firm of Fulbright, Crooker, Freeman & Jaworski in Houston. Some years later, Hutcheson concluded a promising career there to found his own law firm, Hutcheson & Grundy, with his father, brothers and uncle.

Hutcheson's rocketing career as a young trial lawyer was interrupted by World War II, in which he served as Executive Officer of the USS *Swasey*, a destroyer escort, achieving the rank of Lt. Commander in the U.S. Navy. When he returned to Houston, he led his law firm to celebrated success. Hutcheson also became a force in the Texas Republican Party, running for the U.S. Senate and serving twice as its Chairman. In the midst of these pursuits, Hutcheson found time to serve on the Board of Trustees of Kinkaid from 1959 to 1978.

The first-year moot court competition at the University of Texas Law School is named after Hutcheson in recognition of his distinguished career.

# Thomas E. Kelly

Thomas E. Kelly ('49) found that his public speaking experience at Kinkaid served him well in his future political career. Kelly studied and taught geology. In 1954 he joined the Air Force as a special agent in the Office of Special Investigations.

Following release from active duty, Kelly pursued a distinguished career as an exploration geologist and eventually as an executive of Halbouty International in Alaska. He also took a dynamic role in Alaskan politics. He became a highly visible public official, credited with making Alaska a wealthy state (through oil and gas development), and later with native groups, who hired him as a consultant. Kelly was appointed Commissioner of Natural Resources for Alaska in 1967. He remains a Consulting Earth Scientist, and though he calls himself "retired," it is clear that Kelly continues to be an influence in northwest energy exploration.

# Emilie "Mimi" Smith Kilgore

Mimi Smith Kilgore ('53) remembers Kinkaid as a place of academic discipline with superb teachers. She still remembers playing Eliza Doolittle in *Pygmalion* directed by Kinkaid's wonderful Mitzi Johnson.

Kilgore has divided her championing of the arts between the visual and theatrical worlds. She is the President and guiding force behind the Susan Smith Blackburn Prize, founded in 1978 in memory of her sister. Susan ('51), an actress and writer who died much too early, believed that society needed more influence from talented women. Now in its 28th year, the Prize has been a primary force in encouraging and discovering women playwrights. In addition, Kilgore has edited two anthologies of outstanding plays; 2006 will see the publication by the University of Texas Press of *Women Writing Plays: Three Decades of the Susan Smith Blackburn Prize.*

Kilgore has been a trustee of the Alley Theatre, Stages Repertory Theatre, the Contemporary Arts Museum and the Museum of Fine Arts, Houston, among others. For over 25 years, she has been the curator of the Fayez Sarofim Art Collection and in the 1980's she assembled art collections for Texas Commerce Bank.

Smith College awarded her its alumnae medal in 1995, and she was the recipient of the Margo Jones Medal in 2003, awarded annually to someone who has devoted his or her career to the theatre with special emphasis on nurturing playwrights.

# Caroline Wiess Law

Caroline Wiess Law attended Kinkaid in Middle School from 1930 to 1934. She was a daughter of Harry C. Wiess, one of the founders of Humble Oil & Refining, and she graduated from Sarah Lawrence College in 1941. Law and her husband, Theodore Newton Law, founder of Falcon Seaboard Drilling Company and Mid-Continent Airlines, were unparalleled patrons of the City of Houston. For the Museum of Fine Arts, Houston, they purchased an entire city block for construction of the Audrey Jones Beck Building, which beautifully complemented the already existing Caroline Wiess Law Building across the street.

Upon her death in 2003, Law bequeathed $450 million and a staggering art collection to the Museum of Fine Arts, Houston. In addition, she left $50 million to Baylor College of Medicine and M. D. Anderson Cancer Center. Houston stands in awe of her stunning legacy of generosity.

# Christopher M. Little

Christopher M. Little ('59) received a B.A. from Yale University. "I don't think that I would have ended up at Yale without my Kinkaid background and the encouragement of Headmaster John Cooper. I also think that Kinkaid fostered leadership skills and self-confidence that stood me in good stead as I took on more responsibilities."

Little received his law degree from the University of Texas and completed the senior executive program at Stanford University Graduate School of Business. He began a distinguished legal career with Covington & Burling in Washington, D.C., taking a professional sabbatical by serving as Administrative Assistant to Congressman Bob Eckhardt from 1968 to 1970. In 1975, he returned to government service, this time as Assistant General Counsel of the EPA.

In 1976 Katherine Graham called Little to invite him to become Vice President and General Counsel of *The Washington Post*. He went on to become President and Publisher of *The Herald* in Everett, Washington, Senior Vice President of *Newsweek* magazine and then President of *Newsweek* in 1986.

Little retired in 2001 from the Meredith Corporation where he was President of the Magazine and Publishing Groups.

# Mary Nell Jeffers Lovett

Mary Nell Jeffers Lovett ('63) joined the inaugural seventh grade class at Kinkaid's Memorial campus and, as a devoted alumna, has played a significant role in the School's development.

Lovett received her degree in education from the University of Texas and returned to Houston to teach in the Spring Branch Independent School District. With the birth of her daughters (both Kinkaid graduates), she began a 35-year involvement in volunteer endeavors benefiting the Houston community. She developed the expertise in non-profit and volunteer management she utilizes in both professional and volunteer capacities.

In addition to serving as a Founding Director and three-year President of the Board of the Greater Houston Community Foundation, Lovett's outstanding civic leadership has included service as President of the Junior League of Houston, Inc., member of the Alley Theatre Executive Committee, Chairman of the M. D. Anderson Pediatric Scholarship Committee and member of the University of Texas-Houston Health Science Center Development Board, University of Houston School of Social Work Advisory Council, Mayor's Advisory Council on Children and Youth, and the Volunteer Center Board of Directors.

Professionally, she has held the position of Executive Director of Private Sector Initiatives and is currently the Executive Director of Volunteer Services at the University of Texas M. D. Anderson Cancer Center, considered the largest single hospital-based volunteer program in the nation.

A member of Kinkaid's Board of Trustees from 1988 to the present, she became the first woman to chair the Board in 1995, serving four years in that position. For Lovett, "Kinkaid has been an educational home for me – a place where I have been able to make the greatest contribution – a place for which I have deep affection and gratitude."

# Allison Marich

Allison Marich ('77) was the powerhouse of Kinkaid's Forensic and Dramatic Union. Her passion helped the team reach national prominence. She took countless first-place wins in Dramatic Interpretation and went on to compete in the national championships.

Marich studied acting at the University of Houston and moved to California to pursue a career in the theatre. She achieved prominence as an acclaimed actress on stage and in film. "Having grown up in a third-generation theatre family, my desire to be an actress was always in the blood."

Several years ago, however, Marich's professional trajectory was brought to a sudden halt by the tragic death of her brother. Marich, overwhelmed by the intrusion of the media in her grieving family's life, dedicated herself to the advancement of a little-known California Senate Bill, S.B. 262, known as the Personal Privacy Protection Act. In 1998 Governor Pete Wilson signed this bill into law, CA. Civil Code 1708.8. Through passage of this bill, Marich has brought relief to families in anguish and bereavement and created a living memorial to her beloved brother, Michael.

# Jeff Martin

Jeff Martin ('78) was a mainstay of Kinkaid's choir and drama productions, as well as the school cartoonist. He wrote skits and musicals for pep rallies and a humor column for *The Falcon*. Martin's multiple talents pointed him to Harvard University, where he became President of the famed *Harvard Lampoon,* the world's oldest humor magazine distributed on a "just-better-than-quarterly" basis.

In 1983 Martin joined the cadre of staff writers for *Late Night with David Letterman*. He stayed with the show for six years, winning four Emmy Awards for his clever wordplay. Beginning in 1990, Martin developed scripts for the acclaimed TV show *The Simpsons,* an explosive prime-time cartoon directed at adults. He has since been working on independent projects, including *Listen Up* with Jason Alexander.

Martin distinctly remembers Kinkaid as a place where "everyone was encouraged to do everything."

# Carroll Sterling Masterson and Harris Masterson

Harris and Carroll Sterling Masterson ('28) together extended their philanthropy to every avenue of Houston arts. The Mastersons were art collectors of the highest rank. They spearheaded a private drive to raise $72 million for the Gus S. Wortham Theater Center. They served on the Board of the Museum of Fine Arts, Houston for many years, donating their own 700-piece collection of Worcester porcelain in 1984.

After 37 years of marriage, the Mastersons gave their palatial home, Rienzi, to the museum. The house was designed by famed Houston architect John Staub for Masterson's grandfather, Rienzi Melville Johnston, founder of *The Houston Post*. Rienzi is a sanctuary of fine English antiques, paintings, porcelains and precious metalware. Its four acres of magnificent gardens border Buffalo Bayou. The Mastersons' philanthropy extended beyond the arts as well, with generous gifts to hospitals and local charities. They were awarded the National Medal of Arts from President George H. W. Bush.

# Carolyn McCormick

Carolyn McCormick ('77) was already a star when she participated in Kinkaid's drama classes with Mr. Boyd and speech tournaments with Mr. Northup and Mr. Moss. She went on to Williams College and later the American Conservatory Theatre. For a period she worked as a television broadcaster for Channel 39 News in Houston.

McCormick has performed in film, television and live theater. Her many credits include *Enemy Mine, Law and Order, Judging Amy, L.A. Law* and *Star Trek.* She has appeared on Broadway and in repertory across the country. In 2005, McCormick began playing a lead role in the 2econd Stage Theatre's production of Paul Weitz's *Privilege* in New York City.

# Margaret C. McNeese

Margaret C. McNeese ('63) is remembered as "the best horsewoman of our class." She received degrees in both biology and Spanish from Mary Baldwin College, before earning her M.D. from the University of Texas Medical Branch.

Dr. McNeese, today Associate Dean for Student Affairs and Professor of Pediatrics at the University of Texas Medical School, Houston, is a pioneer in the use of mobile clinics and telemedicine. Using state-of-the-art teleconferencing equipment, Dr. McNeese from Houston is able to treat patients in mobile clinics across Texas. Telemedicine provides immediate care for people in remote and disadvantaged areas of the state.

"Many patients in the Valley are not mobile – they don't have access to transportation or to health care, so it makes sense for us to take the clinic to them." McNeese also sees advantages for training medical students, who would otherwise not have exposure to the medical needs of outlying populations in Texas.

Dr. McNeese's work on behalf of children and the underprivileged has earned her countless awards and honors. In 1999 she was the recipient of the Ashbel Smith Distinguished Alumnus Award for The University of Texas Medical Branch School of Medicine, and in 2000 the Children's Advocacy Centers of Texas awarded McNeese their Team Excellence Award for her outstanding leadership.

# THE RIVALRY

*A*fter World War II, a number of parents approached Mrs. Kinkaid about making the School more like an East Coast prep school. Mrs. Kinkaid flatly rejected the idea. She had spent a great deal of time in these famed New England academies, and she had already taken what elements from the East Coast prep schools she had wanted for Kinkaid. No further modifications seemed necessary to her.

Mrs. Kinkaid was furious when a few dissatisfied parents left Kinkaid to found The St. John's School in the fall of 1946. She seldom if ever mentioned St. John's, as though it were nothing more than an unpleasant episode in her history. When John Cooper became Headmaster, however, relations between the two schools warmed. St. John's became Kinkaid's "friendliest enemy," and students from both schools enjoy a fierce rivalry in athletics and arts.

# THE FAMOUS VANISHING OAK TREE

*T*he boys' football team held afternoon practices in the athletic field behind the Richmond Avenue School. There Coach Quinn Connelly, a recent graduate of Rice, was expected to orchestrate plays around a large oak tree. Connelly told Mrs. Kinkaid that the old oak had to be removed so that the boys could practice properly.

"Such a beautiful tree," Mrs. Kinkaid replied, and the subject was dropped.

Connelly returned to the School in the fall of 1934, fully expecting that the tree would be gone. Kinkaid had a good six-man football team, and the boys were ready to drill. He was astounded to find the oak still standing majestically plunk in the middle of the field, ready to ruin every pass and scrimmage.

One weekend Coach Connelly chopped the tree down with the help of several maintenance men who will remain anonymous. It took all night to fell the oak, hew it into small pieces and haul the remains away. Connelly was not at all sure he would have a job the following Monday, but he was certain that Kinkaid's football team would prosper on a proper field.

Quinn Connelly kept his job. Mrs. Kinkaid never mentioned the oak tree. It was said that for years afterward she would walk carefully around the spot where the tree had been as if it were still standing there.

# Kelly Sweeney McShane

"Kinkaid broadened my horizons," said Kelly Sweeney McShane ('83). "I went to college knowing that there was a big wonderful world out there and that I wanted to make a difference in it."

McShane was already making a difference at Kinkaid. She founded the Latin Club and graduated as valedictorian of an eminently scholarly class. McShane attended Harvard, where she graduated magna cum laude, and immediately joined the Peace Corps to work as an agricultural extension agent in Sierra Leone.

Upon returning to the United States, McShane volunteered with several community organizations before joining Hannah House in 1990 as Director of Development and Volunteer Services. Hannah House provides transitional shelter to homeless women. In 1997 McShane needed a change. She entered Georgetown's M.B.A. program and graduated two years later number one in her class.

McShane is currently Executive Director of Community of Hope in Washington, D.C. With a budget of nearly $2 million and a staff of around 40 persons, McShane is determined to break the cycle of poverty in Washington. Community of Hope provides health care, after-school programs, family housing, social services and spiritual support to the city's most vulnerable residents. McShane's "difference" is her indefatigable determination to free people from the shackles of poverty, substance abuse and despair.

# Marshall Merrifield

As an Upper School student, Marshall Merrifield ('78) participated in Kinkaid's program of enlisting older children to help younger children on the playground. His positive intervention and gentle guidance was noticed by faculty and peers. Several years later, after earning his B.A. at Princeton, Merrifield became Founder and President of Playground Partners.

"The whole idea behind Playground Partners was that every child should have fun on the playground, regardless of their skill or grade level, in a safe environment."

Playground Partners teaches parent volunteers how to enhance the school playground experience. The program uses play to reinforce positive social skills and values, such as team-building, conflict resolution and sportsmanship. From his base in San Diego, Merrifield has built alliances with corporate and church sponsors to expand the program.

When not volunteering with Playground Partners, Merrifield is the majority shareholder of General Lock Manufacturing, one of the largest wholesale distributors of commercial security hardware in the United States. Merrifield is also a Co-founder and Board member of Shoreline Studios, a software company that created live animation for sports television, including Fox Sports' glowing hockey puck and the yellow first down line for NFL broadcasts.

## Dinnie Smith Mowery

Dinnie Smith Mowery ('36) graduated from Smith College as a drama major. While her husband, Irl Mowery, served in World War II, Dinnie helped out at Kinkaid, staging shows and creating a memorable "night club" party in the gymnasium.

When Irl returned from service in the Aleutians, he and Dinnie spent several years directing and acting (she as "Dinnie Smith") in regional theatres and summer stock. They spent the 1949-1950 season under contract as producers of Houston Little Theatre before moving to New York.

Dinnie auditioned and became an understudy for both Alice Ghostley and June Carroll in *New Faces of 1952,* in which she made her Broadway debut. After the national tour of *New Faces,* Dinnie returned to Broadway in *Miss Isobel* and *Only in America.* Then she became a leading lady on daytime TV in *Hotel Cosmopolitan* for CBS. When Irl's career dictated various moves across the country, Dinnie chose to stop acting professionally. "A career is nice," she says, "but you can't run your fingers through its hair!"

Upon returning to Houston in 1979, Dinnie resumed her connection with Kinkaid as one of J. Barry Moss's first passengers on his alumni traveling experience.

# Anne Dale Owen and Jane Blaffer Owen

Jane Blaffer Owen ('30) attended school both at Mrs. Kinkaid's house and the Richmond Avenue campus. She remembers Margaret Kinkaid distinctly: "Her will was indomitable, but it wore a velvet glove. She exemplified patience and courage in the pursuit of her goals for excellence."

Owen studied at Bryn Mawr, the Washington School of Diplomacy and the Union Theological Seminary. She founded the English Speaking Union in Houston and became an honorary chaplain to the Ministry for Seamen in Houston. Queen Elizabeth II made Owen a Commander of the British Empire.

Jane Blaffer Owen and her husband, Kenneth Dale Owen, together restored and rebuilt the Indiana town of New Harmony – the "Athens of the West." New Harmony is a utopian community that was founded along the Wabash River in 1824 by Robert Owen, one of the country's great social reformers. The Owens commissioned all aspects of the community's restoration from internationally recognized artists and architects.

New Harmony, originally a spiritual refuge, has become a sanctuary for artists, scientists and scholars worldwide, who find inspiration in communal life. The next generation of the Owen's family interest in New Harmony continues with their daughter Anne Dale Owen ('68) who has continued to support New Harmony's distinct cultural heritage and endowment. Anne Dale Owen has served as CEO of Gulfshore Oil and OOPS Oil, Vice President of Red Geranium Enterprises and trustee of the Robert Lee Blaffer Foundation, the Sarah Campbell Blaffer Foundation and the K. D. Owen Trust.

She has admirably continued the rich tradition of her family's interest in Kinkaid through the activities of her daughter Abigail Owens-Pontez ('08).

# Robbin Parish

Robbin Parish ('61) graduated from the University of Texas and received her M.S. in speech pathology from Our Lady of the Lake College in San Antonio.

"I realized in graduate school that we have strengths and weaknesses in learning, and if taught to our strengths, we will succeed." Parish returned to Houston in 1972 and co-founded the Memorial City Speech, Hearing and Language Center, a private practice to assist adults and children with communicative skills. It was clear from her practice with children that early intervention could help them be successful in the classroom for years to come.

In 1983 Parish founded The Parish School in Houston. This school has been instrumental in identifying and helping children with learning disabilities to establish systems of discovery and study and to succeed in the regular classroom. It is considered one of the finest schools of its kind in the nation.

"Mrs. Kinkaid was an inspiration to me! When I decided to start The Parish School, people called me 'Miss Kinkaid.'"

# Vianei Lopez Robinson

Vianei Lopez Robinson ('85) declared, "Kinkaid students are certainly the best and the brightest students I know of." This is high praise from a woman who was Kinkaid's first Presidential Scholar and the youngest-ever woman graduate of Princeton at the age of 19 in 1988. She then enrolled in the University of Texas Law School as a Vinson & Elkins Scholar. In 1997 Robinson was awarded the Distinguished Young Alumna award and vowed that her teachers at college and law school "couldn't hold a candle to my Kinkaid teachers."

Robinson has a distinguished law practice in Abilene, Texas, and is a frequent author and speaker on employment law issues. She served on the Board of Directors of the State Bar of Texas (2002-2005) and received a Presidential Citation for volunteer service in 2004. She continues to perform in community theatre productions, using the dancing and singing skills she honed at Kinkaid.

# Chuck Scofield

Chuck Scofield ('88) graduated cum laude with high honors from Davidson College in 1992. He launched himself on a world tour to expand his horizons, and while in India, Scofield spent several weeks working with Mother Theresa at Kali Ghat, The Sisters of Charity home for the destitute and dying. In 1995 Scofield, profoundly moved by his experiences abroad, joined the staff of *Who Cares* magazine and helped to launch this national quarterly journal devoted to community service and social activism.

In 1996 Scofield joined the staff of Share Our Strength, the country's leading anti-hunger organization. Scofield has traveled extensively to Ethiopia to promote awareness of the plight of those suffering from drought and hunger. He formed the Ethiopia Relief Fund, raising money for direct assistance. Scofield currently serves as Director of Development of Share Our Strength, responsible for developing new business ventures and raising millions of dollars to launch the organization's strategy to end childhood hunger in America.

Scofield has assisted in writing and editing two highly celebrated books: *The Cathedral Within* and *The Light of Conscience.* Both books highlight the spiritual rewards and inspirational legacy of moral acts in a private life.

# Vernon Scott

For Vernon Scott ('79), theater, dance and music formed the lion's share of his extracurricular activities at Kinkaid. "The focus at Kinkaid seemed to me to be in support of producing Renaissance graduates: well-rounded, athletic, artistic intellectuals – shaping youthful beasts into humble leaders."

Scott went on initially to the University of Virginia to study architecture, another interest of his. But after two years, he switched to the Tisch School of the Arts at New York University. He was offered a scholarship at the Alvin Ailey School, turning it down to complete his undergraduate studies. Thereupon, Scott entered Juilliard and finally immersed himself in performance art.

Scott has been featured as a soloist for years in premier dance companies across the United States and internationally. Most recently he has moved into corporate sales and marketing. His visits to Kinkaid have inspired many students to "follow their bliss."

# Scott Sears

Admiral Scott Sears ('62) left Kinkaid (graduating cum laude) for a full scholarship at the Naval Academy, where he graduated with distinction – sixth in his class of more than a 1,000. Those years gave him "a heart of service." Sears chose to serve on submarines because of the challenging technical demands. He spent 23 years on six different submarines, half of that time beneath the surface of the water.

After initial tours of duty on diesel submarines, Admiral Sears attended M.I.T., where he received a M.S.E.E. in electrical engineering and an E.E. professional degree.

Then, during the Vietnam War, he applied to the nuclear power program. In 1976 Sears navigated the USS *Flying Fish* to the North Pole. From 1983 to 1986 he commanded the USS *Albuquerque,* a brand new Navy submarine. "I am proud to have been part of winning the Cold War," he said.

The Navy selected Sears for its highest rank, Rear Admiral. He led the Naval Undersea Warfare Center for three years before retiring to civilian life.

# Marc J. Shapiro

Marc Shapiro ('65) graduated from Kinkaid with honors. He received a B.A. in economics from Harvard University and went on to Stanford Business School where he graduated first in his class.

Shapiro began his banking career with Texas Commerce Bank in 1972 and five years later was appointed Chief Financial Officer. After J.P. Morgan Chase acquired the bank in 1987, Shapiro became Chief Executive Officer of the statewide organization. In 1997 he moved to New York City to become Vice Chairman for Finance and Risk Management. He retired in 2003 and returned to Houston, turning his financial savvy into a distinguished community service record.

He currently serves as Non-Executive Chairman of Chase Bank of Texas. In addition, he is a director of Burlington Northern Santa Fe Corporation, Kimberly-Clark Corporation and Weingarten Realty Investors.

Energetically committed, Shapiro also acts as Chairman of the Board of Visitors of M.D. Anderson Cancer Center and Co-chairman of the Hobby Center for the Performing Arts, as well as serving on the Boards of Baylor College of Medicine, BioHouston and Rice University.

A Distinguished Alumnus of 2003, Shapiro underscored the values that Kinkaid teaches. "Times change," he said, "but values don't."

# Johnny Sutton

During his years at Kinkaid, Johnny Sutton ('79) learned "to work hard and never, ever give up."

After Kinkaid, Sutton attended the University of Texas on a baseball scholarship to play for the legendary UT baseball coach Cliff Gustafson. Coach Gus produced many stars in his 29 years as head coach, but when asked who his favorite player was, he did not hesitate. He named Johnny Sutton.

"He worked for three years, just waiting to get a chance to play," said Coach Gustafson. "He got in the lineup just before the regional tournament and he ended up the MVP. He was instrumental in helping us win the national championship.

"There are a lot of others I'm proud of, but not in the same way. The way he hung in and worked so hard to earn it really sets him apart."

Sutton's many years at Kinkaid also prepared him well for a career as a trial prosecutor with the District Attorney's Office in Houston. He tried every type of criminal case from theft to kidnapping to capital murder. In 1995 then-Governor George W. Bush picked Sutton to be his Criminal Justice Policy Director, and when the Governor became President, he chose Sutton to lead the Bush-Cheney Transition Team for the U.S. Department of Justice. President Bush appointed him to be the U.S. Attorney for the Western District of Texas in November 2001.

Sutton is also fluent in Spanish, thanks to the outstanding Spanish teachers at Kinkaid. Due to the demographics of the district he serves, which includes over 660 miles of border with Mexico and many Spanish-speaking residents, Sutton is required to speak Spanish routinely. Sutton credits much of his success to his years at Kinkaid.

# Marianne Tatum

For Marianne Tatum ('69), "Kinkaid was my preferred home. My happiest hours were spent playing sports in the gym, rehearsing a show in the auditorium or walking outdoors under the trees."

Tatum's beloved father died when she was only nine. Her love of singing lifted her from her sadness, and Kinkaid gave her many opportunities to perform.

Through the efforts of John Cooper, Tatum was awarded a full scholarship to the Manhattan School of Music. In her senior year she was invited to make her professional debut with Houston Grand Opera as Cherubino in *The Marriage of Figaro*.

On Broadway Tatum first appeared with Yul Brynner in the 1977 revival of *The King and I*. She won a Theatre World Award for her creation of the role of Jenny Lind in *Barnum* and a Drama Desk Nomination for Best Supporting Actress as Milady de Winter in *The Three Musketeers*. She also worked in television in series such as *One Life to Live* and *Law and Order*.

Tatum retired with her family to Tallahassee, Florida, after the events of 9/11, and finished her B.A. in music degree from Florida State University in 2003. She is currently working on her M.A. in the history of American religious thought.

# THE WICKER ROOM

The Wicker Room may have started as a joke between Margaret Kinkaid and her beloved front-office manager Mrs. Yorty. There was a small storeroom at the end of the East Wing of the Richmond Avenue School. It was furnished with a comfortable wicker chaise lounge, a wicker chair, a small table which held her Bible and a bookshelf. When Mrs. Kinkaid retired to The Wicker Room, Mrs. Yorty saw to it that no one disturbed her.

Students only learned of The Wicker Room because on rare occasions a student serving detention might be asked to dust it. One such girl described her visit there as a perfectly lovely chat with Mrs. Kinkaid.

Margaret Kinkaid retired to The Wicker Room when a school issue required deliberate and private reflection. More often than not, she would emerge from the room resolute and peaceful with the current problem solved.

# FIELD DAY'S COOKIE LADY FOR 50 YEARS

*K*inkaid has organized Field Days ever since 1911 when the School was in the house on Elgin Street. In 1937 Field Day funds were used to build a new gym on the Richmond Avenue campus. After that, each Field Day has been dedicated to fundraising for a specific school or community project.

All those who helped with Field Day worked from seven o'clock in the morning to 10 o'clock at night. In the mid-1950's, Betty Dudley opened her famous Cookie and Candy Booth, where she sold her homemade fudge and box loads of Mr. Kegg's divinity. Behind the counter she kept a small cooler with a bottle of wine on ice. This was for the evening, when the crowds died down and the students left and it was time to count the proceeds of the booth.

For the next 50 years, Betty Dudley also kept a shoebox filled with sweets for special people. There was always a package for Mr. Goddard to take home to his mother after she retired. There were treats for Leigh Weld, Henry Freeman and all the maintenance staff. People say Betty Dudley was the last to leave the Field Day playing field. She didn't shut down her booth until the last sweets were sold or given away.

The Cookie and Candy Booth tradition was passed down to Betty Dudley's daughters, but Betty continued to make her special fudge years after the family had graduated.

# Patrick F. Taylor

Patrick F. Taylor ('55) turned an unpromising childhood into a life of unparalleled achievement and magnanimity. Kicked out of his home as a boy, Taylor was among the very first scholarship students to attend Kinkaid. He took full advantage of this opportunity, excelling in math and science. He went on to Louisiana State University, which at the time had no tuition.

Eventually Taylor founded the Circle Bar Drilling Company with Texas oilman John Mecom and later the Taylor Energy Company. One day, at the height of his success, Taylor took the time to speak to a large audience of underprivileged inner-city children. Moved by their collective despair, Taylor spontaneously made an offer to pay the college tuition of every child

there who could maintain a "B" average and steer clear of trouble. This bargain was so roundly successful that Taylor later introduced legislation for a merit-based tuition program in the State of Louisiana. The "Taylor Plan," as it is called, took flight. It now flourishes in more than 19 states.

# Joseph H. Thywissen

Joseph Thywissen ('91) attended Kinkaid "from the Yellow Door until 11th grade, when I decided to go to college one year early. You can't accuse me of skipping out of school, though; I spent 10 more years as a student." Thywissen received a double degree in engineering and physics from Harvey Mudd College. He went on to Harvard for an M.S. and Ph.D. in applied physics.

He left Cambridge for Paris to study under Alain Aspect, a legendary figure in quantum physics. When he returned to North America, he took a position on the faculty at the University of Toronto. Thywissen has published *Atom Manipulation* and *On the Properties of Ultra-Cold Atoms*. His awards and honors testify to how meaningfully he has contributed to scientific research.

David Underwood ('54) remembers at Kinkaid the "warm, nurturing environment. Developing study skills did not hurt either," he adds.

Underwood graduated from Yale University in 1958, attended the Institute of Investment Banking at the Wharton School at the University of Pennsylvania and received an honorary L.L.D. from the University of St. Thomas in 1995. He served for three years in the Army Reserve, attaining the rank of Captain, Armor, USAR, and he was awarded the Army Commendation Medal in 1962, after having been recalled for the Berlin Crisis.

He joined Underwood, Neuhaus & Co. in 1960 and became CEO before the firm was sold. Currently, he serves as a Senior Vice President of Wachovia Securities, LLC and as the President and CEO of Feliciana Corporation. He serves on the Board of The Methodist Hospital and is Chairman of the Board of The Texas Medical Center. He is especially pleased to be a Charter Trustee Emeritus of Phillips Academy, having served as President of that Board of Trustees for 13 years. He is a Life Trustee of Kinkaid where he served as Chairman of the Board in the early 1980's. He is very proud of the fact that to date, he and his father, the late Milton R. Underwood, are the only father-son Chairmen of the Board of Kinkaid. Milton Underwood served as Chairman in the late 1940's. David Underwood has maintained his role as Chairman of Kinkaid Endowment Fund, Inc., helping to ensure Kinkaid's financial strength into the future.

# William D. Van Vorst

William D. Van Vorst ('36) attended Rice University and M.I.T. as a student of chemical engineering. He joined the Faculty of Engineering at UCLA while pursuing his Ph.D. degree. While at UCLA, Van Vorst was honored with several visiting professorships around the world and served as a consultant to UNESCO and UNIDO in Thailand.

Van Vorst explored the use of hydrogen as an internal combustion engine fuel in the early 1970's, far ahead of his time. His record of academic achievement is highly distinguished and decorated with awards. Van Vorst has since become an ardent proponent for hydrogen fuel and a strong advocate for the Clean Air Now foundation. Daimler Chrysler Corporation has recently given the UCLA Engineering Department two of their fuel cell, hydrogen-powered cars for research, and Van Vorst will act as a consultant to the project. In his spare time, he has devoted himself to community causes, such as the Boy Scouts and Little League.

Was Kinkaid a factor? "I think the fine courses in math and chemistry – and the excellent instruction therein – started it all."

# Damon Wells

Damon Wells ('54) recalls: "I first saw Mrs. Kinkaid in 1942 when she came to our kindergarten class to urge us to buy U.S. war bonds. She used the word 'stewardship' which I would hear from her many times again in connection with campus Red Cross or Community Chest drives."

Wells left Kinkaid to graduate with high honors from Yale (B.A.), Oxford (M.A.) and Rice (Ph.D.). He founded the Damon Wells Investment Company, which has become a preeminent financial business. Wells also established and endowed the Damon Wells Fellowship at Kinkaid. This program brings prominent leaders to the School to spend time talking with students. Wells is proud of this Fellowship, which gives Kinkaid students a better understanding of the world beyond the classroom.

"I think the program has fulfilled my goals and, more importantly, that Mrs. Kinkaid would be pleased."

## Temple Williams

Temple Williams ('83) found a love for the arts while at Kinkaid. He attended Northwestern University and then ventured to California to pursue an acting career. Having distinguished himself in film, he moved back to Chicago to join the Lookingglass Theatre Company, an acclaimed and award-winning troupe of Northwestern alumni.

Williams returned to Los Angeles to further his television and film career.

He worked for Dreamworks, Disney, Miramax and MTV, among others. Williams finally settled with MTV, where he is Senior Vice President / Executive in charge of production. He oversees production on all series on the West Coast, including *The Osbournes, Newlyweds: Nick and Jessica, Jackass, The Real World, Road Rules* and more.

His advice? "Be open to anything."

**DECEMBER 1924**
The School opens on Richmond Avenue and Graustark Street, and the first Open House is held

**1924**
The Hogg Family donates site of Camp Logan to city of Houston, renamed Memorial Park

**1928**
The Houston Municipal Airport opens

**1930**
Population of Houston exceeds 292,350

**1930**
William Kinkaid begins teaching at the School and stays for over 20 years

**1934**
Four scholarship students are accepted from the Houston public school system as many public school administrators know of Mrs. Kinkaid and applaud her determination to make scholarships available to worthy students citywide

**SEPTEMBER 1934**
Football Coach Quinn Connelly cuts down the notorious tree that Mrs. Kinkaid did not want to part with to make more room for a football field

**1938**
Construction of Kinkaid's "Little Gym" completed for $38,000

**1938**
First graduating class from Kinkaid to proceed on to college is composed of five girls

**1939**
Houston becomes the third largest port in tonnage in the U.S.

**1940**
Graduating class of nine seniors includes six boys

**1940**
Kinkaid becomes first school in Houston to offer a full college preparatory course of 12 years

**SPRING 1966**
The Anderson-Arnold Science & Survival Center is dedicated, with classroom / lab and amphitheatre lecture hall above ground and stocked fallout shelter beneath

**1967**
The miniskirt hits high fashion

**1968**
Martin Luther King and Robert Kennedy are assassinated

**JULY 20, 1969**
Neil Armstrong walks on the moon

**1969**
Enrollment at Kinkaid jumps to 970 with the high school numbering over 300 for the first time

**1970**
Lower School creates "open" classrooms with teachers organized into "teams"

**1970**
First Career Lab is created by Mrs. Joan Bowers where students work with businesses and professional leaders

**1970**
First time Kinkaid students are selected into *Who's Who*

**1970**
Boys win the SPC title in basketball

**JANUARY 1971**
First Interim Term program starts with great success

**1971**
Moran Library is dedicated as a gift from John and Rose Moran

Dedication of The Kinkaid Middle School Building

**1989**
First student-run Fine Arts Board is organized

**1990**
Each division of the School begins having a Parents' Night

**1992**
Middle School moves to new building and fifth grade becomes part of Middle School

**1992**
The Kinkaid Backyard is dedicated

**1992**
Establishment of Papadopoulos Biology Endowment to bring renowned speakers to Kinkaid

**1993**
Mr. Cooper dies

**1994**
Kinkaid wins National Forensic competition

**1995**
Opening of Melcher Gym and weight room

**1995**
Dedication of Wheless Lobby and offices

**1996**
Boys and girls lacrosse take State

**MAY 1996**
Glenn Ballard retires and Don North becomes new Headmaster

**1996**
Barnhart Trophy Hall created

**1997**
Long-range planning process begins

**1998**
First Annual Kinkaid Alumni Association Golf Tournament, now called the Zack Semander Memorial Tournament

**1997**
Girls field hockey team is undefeated and wins SPC

**1998**
Start of Kinkaid's first swim team

**1998**
Book Fair moves to Melcher Gym

**1904**
Actual year school opened in Mrs. Kinkaid's home

**1906**
School reopens after one-year hiatus due to the birth of William Kinkaid

**1910**
Cottage on Elgin and San Jacinto Streets becomes two stories, making room for many children wanting to enroll

**1910**
Population of Houston nears 78,000

**1911**
First Field Day

**1914**
Start of World War I

**1916**
First attempt to organize a Kinkaid football team

**1917**
Kinkaid adds sixth grade and is considered "complete"

**1918**
Governor William P. Hobby signs bill giving Texas women right to vote

**1920**
Population of Houston grows to 138,276

**1920**
Tuition for first and second graders is $90 per year with cost increasing in $10 increments per year to $130 for a student in sixth grade

**1920**
The purple and gold colors of Kinkaid are adopted

**1921**
Original school song "Kinkaid, My Own Kinkaid" is written by Charlotte Williams Darby and Elizabeth Law

**1923**
First school newspaper, *The Kinkaid Almanac,* is published

**JUNE 25, 1924**
First meeting of Board of Trustees: Burke Baker, R. L. Blaffer, W. L. Clayton, E. L. Neville and H. C. Wiess

**SEPTEMBER 1959**
Parking stickers are issued for the first time to faculty and students

**1960**
Kinkaid's first Cum Laude Society is established

**FALL 1960**
Jennifer Smith is crowned Kinkaid's first Homecoming Queen

**1960**
For the first time in four years, Kinkaid soundly beats St. John's in football – 26-6

**1961-1962 SCHOOL YEAR**
The first foreign students sponsored by A.F.S. come to Kinkaid from Sweden and Germany

**OCTOBER 1962**
The Cuban Missile Crisis

**1962**
The Spaulding Method of Reading instituted in Lower School

**1963**
Soccer becomes a Kinkaid varsity sport

**1963**
200,000 march on Washington in support of Civil Rights

**NOVEMBER 22, 1963**
President John F. Kennedy is assassinated

**1964**
The Houston Astrodome is built

**1964**
George W. Bush becomes ninth grade Class Vice President

**1964**
Opening of the Lower School Arts and Recreation Building

**FALL 1965**
The high school day is lengthened 20 minutes to allow for lab time or study hall

**FALL 1965**
507 boys and 409 girls are enrolled at Kinkaid

**FALL 1980**
Three St. John's football players are "kidnapped" on game day and returned after the Kinkaid pep rally

Kinkaid wins 20-0

**1980**
Glenn Ballard inaugurates Grandparents' Day and the Annual Kindergarten Dad's Breakfast

**1980**
Graduation moves from front campus to athletic field

**1981**
Class scrapbooks started

**1982**
First Annual Middle School Science Fair

**1983**
First Kinkaid auction held

**1983**
First Alumni Phonathon

**1984**
First Columbiana Award is given to honor excellence in teaching

**SPRING 1986**
Boys track, tennis and golf are SPC Champions

**1986**
First time Kinkaid band makes All-State

**1987**
Girls win the SPC titles in golf, tennis and softball

**1987**
Start of Weiner Fellowship Program

**1989**
Alumni Association is revived

**1989**
Kinkaid's first "official" school nurse hired – Bonnie Hetrick

**1989**
*Pen Power,* a magazine featuring writing by middle school students, has its first issue

**1989**
Lacrosse is offered as a Kinkaid sport for the first time

**1957**

The Richmond Avenue property is sold to Seventh Day Adventists for approximately $400,000 and Kinkaid moves to Memorial

**NOVEMBER 1957**

Launch of *Sputnik,* the first space satellite

**1958**

The election of Mr. and Miss Falcon begins

**1958**

Kinkaid girls volleyball team wins A.T.P.S. trophy for the fourth consecutive year, losing only one game

**SUMMER 1958**

Construction of the cafeteria is completed

**1958**

Kinkaid theatre stages *Hamlet,* its first Shakespearean play

**1959**

The endowment fund is created and The Fondren Foundation kicks off the first Endowment Fund Drive with a challenge gift of $40,000

**1959**

First alumni newsletter published

**1959**

Trustees discuss need for school uniforms after hearing that "the uniforms at St. John's look better than the clothes of the Kinkaid students"

Some Board members strongly disagree, and the issue is tabled until 1962

**1959**

Harris County population grows to more than one million

Kinkaid opens to 889 students with waiting lists for every grade except 11th and 12th

**1975**

A musical instrument program for Lower School is initiated and band begins in Middle School

**SUMMER 1976**

The first Kinkaid-HISD Engineering Math Science Summer Institute is held

**1976**

Kinkaid tests more than 1,200 children for 140 openings and enrollment reaches 1,178

**1976**

All eighth grade students are required to take Latin

**1976**

The Foster Parker all-weather track is built

**APRIL 6, 1976**

In Kinkaid's 70th year three buildings are dedicated: John H. Blaffer Performing Arts Center, M.D. Anderson Home Arts Center and Frank P. Sterling Science Center

**1978**

John Cooper announces his retirement after 28 years of service

**JULY 19, 1978**

The Tintoretto painting, *The Baptism of Christ,* which hung in Kinkaid's main hall is stolen, and its $125,000 insurance value becomes part of Kinkaid's permanent endowment

**1978**

The search committee chooses Glenn Ballard as the next Headmaster

**1978**

KOCI is begun by Alicia Woodhams

**1979**

Photography Department begins under David Veselka

**FEBRUARY 7, 1979**

The Abercrombie Student Center is dedicated as a place for students to study or chat during free time

**MARCH 2002**

Final drama performance in Blaffer Auditorium – *Bye Bye Birdie*

**2002**

First meeting of Greater Houston Area Community of Concern to address the issue of drug and alcohol use

**MARCH 19, 2003**

The Iraq War begins

**2003**

First Character Education Director hired

**2003**

New construction at Kinkaid is completed: The Kinkaid Theatre and Center for Student Life, Fine Arts and Administration

**2004**

Kinkaid band performs in China

**2004**

Opening of the new theatre honors Doc Bill Glick with *What's Up, Doc?*

**2004**

Devastating Indian Ocean tsunami kills thousands

Upper School students organize successful tsunami relief fundraiser

**2004**

Drama program ranked in top three high school programs, and members travel to the Edinburgh Festival to perform

**SPRING 2005**

First baseball game under the new lights on Sanders Field

**2005**

Completion of the $47 million Capital Campaign

**SEPTEMBER 2005**

Hurricane Katrina batters New Orleans, Mississippi and Alabama

Kinkaid welcomes 78 evacuated students

**2005-2006**

Kinkaid's Centennial Celebration

**DECEMBER 7, 1941**
The Japanese bombing of Pearl Harbor

**1942**
The Kinkaid bus introduced due to gas rationing

**1945**
World War II ends

**1946**
St. John's School opens

**1946**
First Kinkaid yearbook published

**1948**
Kinkaid has an all-male graduating class

**1950**
Mrs. Kinkaid retires and John Cooper becomes Headmaster

**JUNE 1950**
A new gymnasium is built

**DECEMBER 20, 1951**
Mrs. Kinkaid dies in an automobile accident

**1951**
Kinkaid loses first-ever football game against St. John's – 49-6

**1951**
Kinkaid's first Book Fair

**1952**
A summer school program is begun

**1952**
Mitzi Johnson hired as first full-time professional theatre teacher – her first production is *Pygmalion*

**1954**
Due to overcrowding, plans to move Kinkaid to new Alief site begin

Change required when city council adopts plans for the Southwest Freeway which is to cut through part of the site

**1955**
A plan for faculty pensions is approved

**1956**
The Memorial site is approved by the Board

**1971**
The distinguished Wells Fellowship is established, bringing guest speakers to Kinkaid

**1972**
Kinkaid is the only private school in the state named a "demonstration school" by Texas Education Agency, honored for its open concept and team teaching in Lower School, and Interim Term and Career Lab in Upper School

**1972**
The Nixon Watergate scandal grabs headlines

**1972**
Kinkaid enrolls 1,147 students and an additional building is completed for the Lower School

**1972**
First eighth grade trips to Washington, D.C.

**1973**
The Vietnam War comes to an end

**OCTOBER 1973**
The Holcombe Library in Lower School, a gift of the Crosswell family, is dedicated

**1973**
Extension of San Felipe beyond Voss makes access to campus much easier

**JANUARY 1974**
The Century 21 Campaign begins

**FALL 1974**
Gary McMillan begins as the new head football coach and has the first undefeated and untied varsity football team in Kinkaid's history

**1974**
S.O.K. (Spirit of Kinkaid) is created with 150 members

**1975**
Faculty salaries are raised to an average of $12,500

**1998**
Varsity football wins SPC for second consecutive year

**APRIL 1999**
Field Day marks first major event in the new Barnhart Stadium

**FEBRUARY 2000**
First Lower School International Fair features France, Japan, Mexico and Nigeria

**FEBRUARY 2000**
Kinkaid orchestra travels to Boston to work with two internationally acclaimed conductors, Boston Philharmonic director Benjamin Zander and Harvard Orchestra director James Yannatos

**2000**
Kinkaid Children's Theatre program is developed by Patty Edwards

**NOVEMBER 2000**
Book Fair celebrates 50th anniversary

**JANUARY 2001**
Lower School moves to the new Friedkin Family Building

**FALL 2001**
KLS-TV started in Lower School

**SEPTEMBER 11, 2001**
Terrorist attacks on the World Trade Center in New York and The Pentagon in Washington, D.C.

**FALL 2001**
Boys cross-country wins SPC for the first time

**2001**
Swimming wins SPC for the first time

**2001**
Girls lacrosse wins State Championship

**2002**
School core values adopted – kindness, honesty, respect and responsibility

**JUNE 2002**
Kinkaid begins construction on third building project of the Capital Campaign – Center for Student Life, Fine Arts and Administration

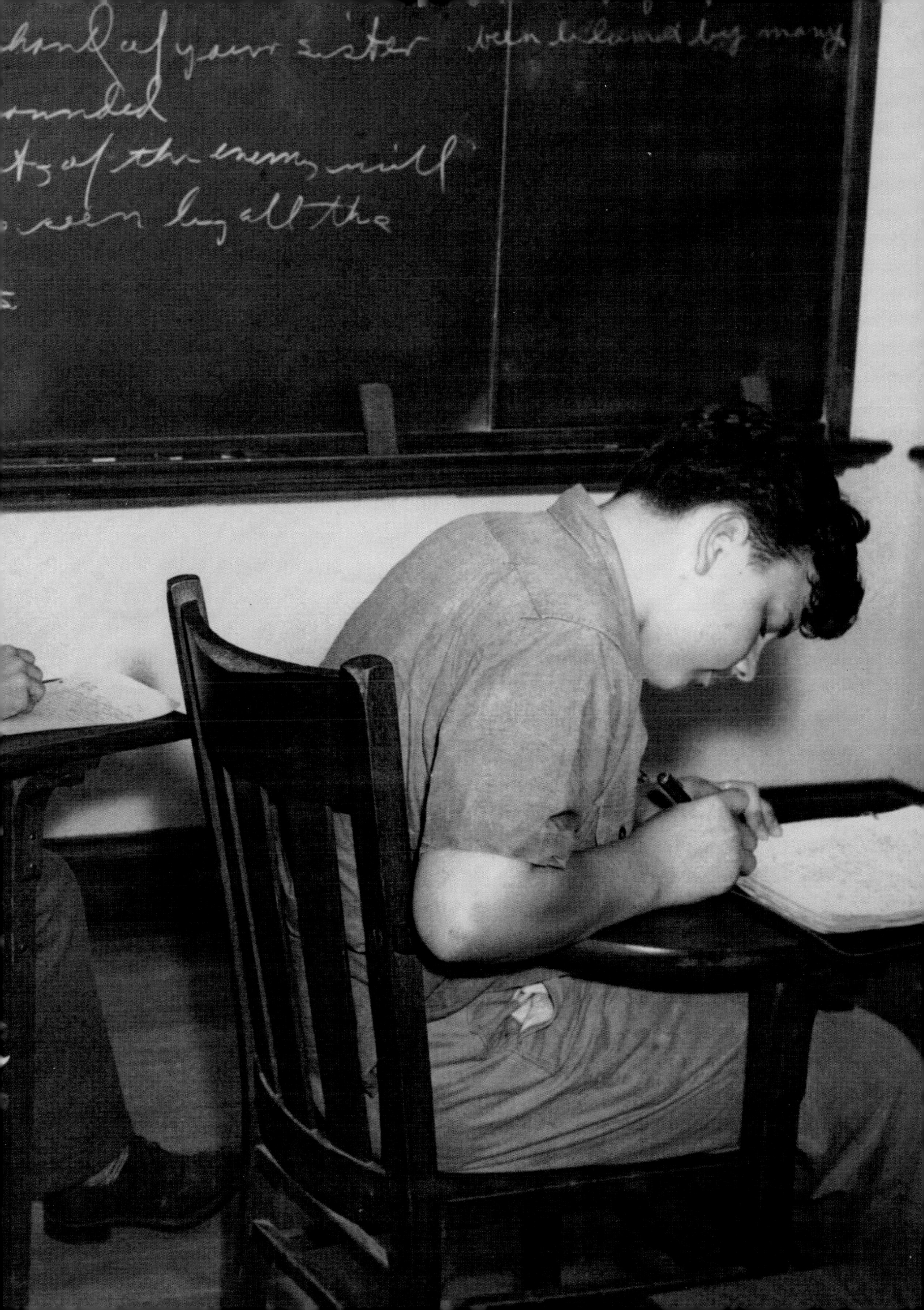

# Fred Angerstein

Fred Angerstein was playing his tuba professionally with the orchestras of the Houston Grand Opera and Houston Ballet when Headmaster John Cooper talked him into starting a band program at Kinkaid. He worked part-time in 1972, but came on board full-time two years later to find that his fledgling "band" of five fourth and fifth graders had swelled to 16 and now included Upper School students. The Band Department had no instruments back then, so one can only imagine Angerstein's amazement when the Dad's Club announced at the beginning of school that the Kinkaid band would be playing at every home football game! They did manage to play at some of the games in those early years, and today the band is a fixture at Falcon games. Band was the first performing arts class to be offered during the school day, and now the award-winning Kinkaid band has over 200 members in Middle and Upper Schools. Kinkaid's band has been invited to play for audiences in faraway places such as Europe and China.

# G'Ann and Tom Boyd

In 1955 John Cooper persuaded Tom Boyd to leave his post as teacher and Technical Theater Director at the University of Houston and come to Kinkaid where he could head up his own Theater Department and try his hand at directing. Boyd saw the job as an "experiment," but it was such a successful one that, in many ways, it became his life for 30 years.

Boyd married G'Ann, a young dancer and choreographer. At first she assisted Tom at Kinkaid part-time because she was with her own musical comedy company. It soon became apparent that Tom and G'Ann Boyd were a first-rate team, and Mr. Cooper hired G'Ann as a full-time member of the department. From that time on, drama flourished at Kinkaid.

The Boyds felt that athletes, "bookworms" and those who were very shy belonged in the theater right along with students of a more artistic bent who thrived in the spotlight. It was not uncommon during a Boyd rehearsal to see a 200-pound linebacker trying to learn a dance routine while simultaneously singing the lyrics from a Broadway musical!

Tom and G'Ann Boyd's approach to the arts – that there was a place for everyone who wanted to participate, and that the important thing was to learn to appreciate the arts through that participation – formed the basis for the renowned Fine Arts Department Kinkaid has today.

# Jan Braden

In 1964 Jan Braden was fresh out of college when she came to Kinkaid eager to begin her coaching career. A fine athlete herself, she coached both Middle School and varsity teams for three seasons each year. She left Kinkaid in 1978 to pursue other interests, but Glenn Ballard persuaded her to return in 1984 as the School's first Girls' Athletic Director, a position she held until her retirement.

When she took over the girls' program, Braden knew that she had work to do to bring it to parity with the boys' athletic program. She was an administrator of many talents. She assembled a stellar coaching staff, served as a wise mentor for young coaches and attended every game in every sport she could. Because she had a particular love for the game of field hockey, she continued to coach the varsity team, which won an impressive nine SPC championships under her leadership.

Braden would say that good coaching is more about the players, their development of skills, teamwork and character than it is about winning. Every player on Braden's teams played to win, but win or lose, her teams were known throughout the conference for their fine sportsmanship. Many players on Braden's field hockey teams went on to play in college, more than eight playing on collegiate Division I teams. Particularly gratifying, Braden admits, is that several of the girls she coached have become coaches themselves.

When Jan Braden retired in 2003, girls' athletics at Kinkaid had come into its own. Now, the girls' teams are talented and deep; the records at SPC are impressive. "The players deserve the credit," Braden would say – but it is her legacy that has made the girls' program what it is today.

# Ann Tharp Clifford

Head of the English Department from the
early 1930's until her retirement in 1970,
Ann Tharp Clifford shared Margaret
Kinkaid's determination that each child in
the School become more than proficient
at insightful reading and clarity of written
expression. In those days before computers or even self-correcting typewriters,
students were expected to turn in error-
free papers – on the day and at the time
they were due. They were expected
also to read constantly and to read "The
Greats": Shakespeare, Homer, Melville,
Hawthorne and Conrad, among others.

Mrs. Clifford was remembered as a
gifted mentor by a host of younger teachers, among them J. Barry Moss, who
often said that he learned every refine-
ment of teaching expertise from her, not
the least of which was never to accept
sloppy work from any Kinkaid student.

# Barbara Cooney

Barbara Cooney began teaching in Middle School some 30 years ago under Art Goddard, who was already a legendary principal and teacher of history. Little did we suspect then that Cooney would create a legend herself – the "Cooney note taking method."

Two Kinkaid alumni who graduated in different decades and had never met were sitting next to one another in a law school class. When the professor began his lecture, both students began to write furiously. At a pause, one student looked at the other's notes and began to chuckle. He held up his own paper on which the notes were done in exactly the same manner as those of his classmate. "Don't tell me you went to Kinkaid!" the first student exclaimed.

"I sure did," his neighbor said, "and I had Miss Cooney, too!"

The subject matter of Cooney's ancient history course is often fascinating to sixth graders, but long after they have forgotten what pharaoh built which pyramid, they remember how to determine what is relevant in a paragraph and how to transfer that information to a note card. It was no surprise when Cooney won The Columbiana Award for Excellence in Teaching, for her knowledge of middle school children is prodigious, and she continues to be admired by both her students and their parents.

# A TRADITION OF SERVICE BEGINS

*M*rs. Kinkaid was concerned that her rather affluent students were unaware of how people were suffering through the Great Depression years. She launched a community service initiative. Food baskets were prepared for needy families at Thanksgiving and Christmas. Children were encouraged to make toys and to donate learning materials to churches and schools in afflicted parts of Houston.

This tradition continues today at Kinkaid. Toys, foods and practical supplies are collected for less fortunate families as part of every holiday season.

# FOR THE BOYS

*T*hose of us who were in school that infamous day will always remember that Margaret Kinkaid called all the students together in the big study hall to hear the broadcast when President Roosevelt announced that the attack on our naval forces in Pearl Harbor marked the beginning of World War II. Those of us in the right age bracket knew that we could probably not graduate with our class, for we would be inducted into the armed forces as soon as we reached the age of 18.

Mrs. Kinkaid and the teaching staff generously arranged that the boys who were affected could double-up on their courses and have enough credits to earn their diplomas early. So when my class of 1945 graduated, I was in the midst of my training at the naval base in San Diego. I will always be grateful to the School for making it possible for me to go immediately into college when the war ended.

JOHN M. LEGARE, CLASS OF 1945

# A.W.O.L.

*During my years as a student at Kinkaid, I can remember only one time when I was punished for bad behavior. My freshman year in high school, yearbook pictures were scheduled to be taken right after school. My best friend and I thought it imperative that we look absolutely gorgeous in ours. We felt it most necessary to wash our hair beforehand. The best way to do this, we thought, was to skip gym class (the last period in the day) and to walk down Graustark Street to her house at the corner of Bissonnet Street and South Boulevard. This we did.*

*On returning to school, we saw parked outside the gym my grandmother's car. She and an out-of-town guest had come to meet me and were standing with Mrs. Kinkaid. Needless to say, Mrs. Kinkaid was not happy when I was nowhere to be found.*

*We met my grandmother's guest and when they left, Mrs. Kinkaid confronted us. She told us that we would have to be punished, that we could not attend gym for a week, and that we would have to go to study hall instead. My friend was sad. She was very athletic – a state championship tennis player. I was thrilled. I hated gym.*

*I am sorry to say that the yearbook pictures were not very good!*

FRANCITA STUART KOELSCH ULMER, CLASS OF 1949

*Francita wrote the 50-year history of Kinkaid when she was in her early twenties.
She was instrumental in obtaining a Texas Historical Marker for the School.*

# Joyce Crowl

It might seem unusual to describe a teacher of second grade as "formidable," but in Joyce Crowl's case, the adjective fit. Crowl, who never completely lost her British accent, was hired by John Cooper in 1963. He recognized her as a caring and energetic expert in Lower School, and over the years, she proved to be as adept at counseling young parents as she was at handling their children, who adored her. A once naughty boy, now in his thirties, says, "Even when we didn't meet her expectations, which was pretty often for some of us, we knew she cared and wanted us to succeed."

During Crowl's 22-year tenure, the Lower School experimented with the "open classroom" concept and, after the walls went up again, instituted team teaching. She says she learned a great deal in the open classroom years, but is surer that team teaching is a sound educational practice. One aspect of being on a team that she particularly enjoyed was getting the chance to teach math to the whole second grade.

Crowl was the first recipient of Kinkaid's Columbiana Award for Excellence in Teaching, and she was a very popular choice; her devotion to her students and her love for the School were evident in all she did.

## Pat Foley

In 1970, Pat Foley became Kinkaid's first visual artist-in-residence. John Cooper had seen some of his bronze sculptures and had heard from collectors interested in new artists that Foley was "a young man to watch" in the art world. The promise of his own studio space attached to his own classroom appealed to Foley, and he began a teaching career at Kinkaid that lasted more than 20 years.

Not much about Foley was conventional. Resident in his studio for many years was a large yellow cat, "Kitty Dammit," who benevolently tolerated students as well as Foley's occasional attempts to persuade him not to nap on pieces of artwork. Sometimes Foley brought his dog with him to the studio, but neither animal seemed to interfere in the least with the quite extraordinary art that was being produced, either by Foley or his students.

After a few years, Foley was asked to offer, in addition to his regular art classes, a class in architecture, a subject that he thought might be of little interest to high school students. Instead, it was a great success and remained one of the most popular electives open to juniors and seniors. Through the years, Foley maintained his own career as a sculptor, and he did many pieces which grace our present campus. His students remember him as inspirational, iconoclastic and very hard working. Every one of them got a taste of the discipline and sense of purpose required to produce a work of art; and today they say that they learned to appreciate and understand art – all kinds of art – because of who Foley was and what he taught them.

# John and Caro Ann Germann

John Germann came to Kinkaid in 1967. Generations of Germann's students have learned to share his love of history, while groaning at his puns and becoming fascinated by his detailed accounts of little-known signers of the U.S. Constitution. An avid philatelist, Germann has firsthand knowledge of almost every post office in Texas. His interest in, and knowledge about, World War II astounded the students who accompanied him on a tour of European battlegrounds during a recent Interim Term trip.

Former students remember how Germann's enthusiasm for the abandoned details of history made the study of it doubly fascinating. In addition to chairing the History Department and the Weiner Fellowship Program, Germann continues to sponsor Kinkaid's Prep Bowl team. The announcement in 1985 of Germann's winning the Columbiana Award for Excellence in Teaching was met with a standing ovation from students and faculty alike.

Caro Ann Germann joined her husband at Kinkaid in 1978. She came to work part-time as an assistant in third grade, but as an experienced teacher, she was called on to substitute whenever one was needed in Lower School. As time allowed, she did volunteer work in the Lower School library, a place that became her bailiwick some three years later when she became a full-time librarian. When Glenn Ballard asked Germann to take over the running of the library in Lower School, she agreed to pursue her M.S. in library science along with her new duties.

Germann used to teach young students how to use the library's card catalogue; today, she teaches them how to access books using computers and on-line searches. Her library remains among the busiest and liveliest place in the School.

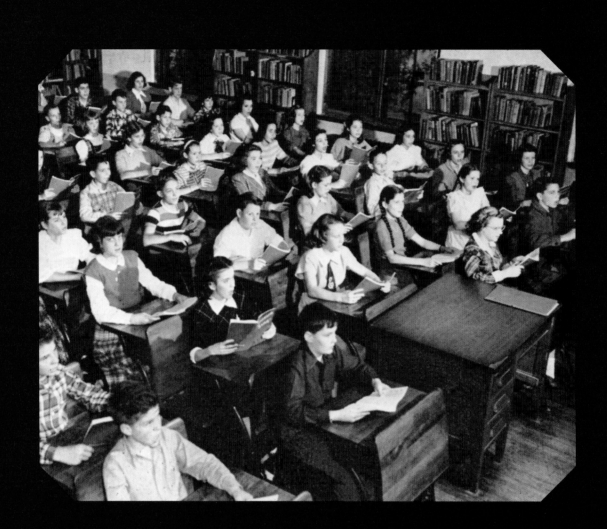

# Arthur Goddard

Art Goddard was a teacher and administrator at Kinkaid for 42 years. Mrs. Kinkaid hired him in 1946 and said, after he had been at the School only one semester, that he was one of the most talented teachers she had ever come across. His patience with, and understanding of, middle school students was legendary. He became the Principal of Middle School very early in his career because Mrs. Kinkaid so admired his handling of a disciplinary situation involving a truculent 12-year-old boy. It was his pleasure, Goddard said, to teach the son of that boy many years later: "A fine young man, just as his father was," Goddard remembered.

Goddard taught history throughout his career. Generations of his students remember the vivid accounts of his experiences with Patton's Army in Europe and his understanding of the tide of events that shaped the outcome of that war. American history had been a lifelong interest for Goddard, but when he came to Kinkaid, he was expected to teach Texas history as well – a history he knew next to nothing about. He said that Mrs. Kinkaid's own interest in Texas history whetted his appetite. He soon found the history of Texas, and that of the "Old 300" first families of Texas, especially fascinating when he discovered that Mrs. Kinkaid's forebears were part of that group.

Goddard was honored to receive the Columbiana Award for Excellence in Teaching in 1987. After his retirement, he continued to visit the School often and to have lunch once a month with a lively group of retired Kinkaid teachers. Only a few months before his death in 2004, Goddard completed a book about his life; Kinkaid is very much a part of that memoir.

## Esther Holt

Esther Holt was hired some 29 years ago by Leigh Weld to run a cleaning crew that maintained all the School buildings in the evenings. She was so good at it that she was soon asked to work days in the Yellow Door building of prekindergarten. Though mothers of toddlers sometimes found it hard to believe, Holt loved keeping things neat and clean for our youngest students. It was difficult five years later for Athletic Director Dan Hart to persuade her to come to work for him in the gym. Holt has been a mainstay in the athletic area for over 20 years, although she works now primarily with girls' sports. She knows every nook and cranny of the gyms, the locker rooms and the athletic offices.

Holt first gets to know students in Lower School, and it has been a great pleasure for her to see them grow into responsible young adults – some of whom now have children in Lower School!

# Ava T. Hooks

An experienced math and science teacher, Ava T. Hooks began teaching both subjects at Margaret Kinkaid's little school on Elgin Street. Small and quick, Mrs. Hooks was much admired by pupils who in the early years had to trot to keep up with her on the "nature walks" she felt beneficial "to clear the mind for study."

After some years, Mrs. Kinkaid hired a science teacher, and Mrs. Hooks was able to concentrate on teaching math, a subject to which she wanted very much to attract more young ladies. She took particular delight in hearing that some of her female students had gone on to become physicians or engineers. "I knew that girl had a fine mind!" Mrs. Hooks would say with a smile. Mrs. Hooks put up with absolutely no nonsense in the classroom, and her sometimes abrupt manner frightened students. But once they encountered her patient willingness to explain a concept in as many ways, and for as many times, as it took them to grasp it, that fear subsided.

The bond between Mrs. Kinkaid and Mrs. Hooks was a strong and trusting one, partly because they shared a commitment to the Christian Science Church. When Mrs. Kinkaid was absent from the School, Mrs. Hooks was in charge. When the School moved to the Richmond Avenue campus, Mrs. Hooks became head of the Math Department. She was still teaching with undiminished energy and enthusiasm at the time of her death in 1962.

# Mary Jones

In 1952 Mary Jones came to Kinkaid as a part-time assistant teacher in Lower School. She loved the young children and seemed to be unfailingly patient with them. Carl Reed, then Principal of Upper School, thought that perhaps her kind manner would put at ease some of the young people applying to Kinkaid, and so he asked Jones to take charge of admissions testing. Almost immediately, he asked her to help out with some of the work in his office – and before she knew it, she was working at Kinkaid full-time.

Jones continued to work in Lower School for many years, but she kept her Upper School job as well. Perhaps most surprisingly, she rode the school bus home every afternoon as the person-in-charge for more than 30 years! Every time a parent, exasperated with the three or four children in her carpool, would exclaim to Jones, "How can you stand to ride with dozens of those noisy children every single day!" She would smile her serene smile and reply in her calm voice. She enjoyed riding the bus because she got to know the children outside the classroom. She found them to be, more often than not, just as delightful as their parents!

By the time of her retirement, the school bus was a thing of the past, and Jones had acquired a driver's license. Her optimism, her ready smile and her steadfast belief in the goodness of every student endeared her to generations of Kinkaidians.

# Katherine Leathem

Katherine Leathem taught science in Middle School when she came to Kinkaid in 1978. Her particular interest was biology, but her students received a solid foundation in various aspects of science along with an appreciation for the natural world and a great respect for proper laboratory procedure.

When there was an opening for a biology teacher in Upper School, Glenn Ballard persuaded her to take it, and she has taught honors biology to freshmen and advanced placement biology to seniors for many years now.

Leathem is passionate about ecology and eco-systems. She recognized that in the area beyond our football field there was a place that could be developed as an outdoor classroom; there, students could experience firsthand the ecology of a bayou and its surroundings. She garnered support among her colleagues and proposed The Kinkaid Backyard, a project several years in the making. It is now so successful that the area has been officially dedicated as a nature preserve. Her classes, and those of science teachers from all divisions of the School, as well as art and photography students can be found at various times during the school year using our Backyard classroom.

As dedicated to her students as she is to the material she teaches, Leathem is a hard and meticulous worker who expects the same from her students – and she usually gets it!

In 1989 Leathem earned the Columbiana Award for Excellence in Teaching.

# Georgia and Eddie Leonard

For generations of alums, it is impossible to remember their Kinkaid days without thinking of Georgia and Eddie Leonard. Georgia's smile behind the cash register and Eddie's friendly wave every morning as we turned into the front gates are as much a part of the Kinkaid experience as excellent teachers and small classes. Thursdays were "Eddie's fried chicken" days; they attracted not only students and faculty, but often our postman and more than a few parents to the cafeteria as well.

Georgia Morgan came to the School in 1962 as an employee of the firm that provided Kinkaid's cafeteria service. She was such a favorite that she could persuade even the most reluctant second grader to eat his vegetables! Eddie Leonard, who had trained as a cook in the Army, joined the cafeteria staff in 1963. He "connected" with students, too, as someone with whom they could always feel comfortable. After working side by side for a few years, Eddie and Georgia married, and they have been inseparable in the minds of Kinkaidians ever since.

In 1982 the School took over the operation of the cafeteria, and Georgia and Eddie were everybody's choice to run it. They assembled a staff that included Georgia's sister, Barbara, and their son, Eddie, Jr., for many years.

As the School grew, so did the morning traffic on San Felipe. Headmaster Glenn Ballard asked Eddie to "police things" on the street and act as a crossing guard for the children. In 2003 Eddie was nominated by an alumnus for the Channel 2 "Sunshine Award." The entire school gathered on the football field on a beautiful October morning to take part in this special award ceremony.

The Leonards' combined years of service to Kinkaid stood at an unprecedented 79 when Georgia retired in 2002. The outpouring of love for her and appreciation for her work was a reflection of the warmth and goodness she has given to Kinkaid over the years.

The school community was deeply saddened when Eddie Leonard, whose ready smile and good cooking were still very much a part of Kinkaid, suddenly passed away shortly before completion of this book. Students, parents and passers-by on San Felipe will sorely miss this fine man who was, as one youngster put it, "the friendliest, best crossing guard in the whole world."

# Garry McMillan

In 1974 trustees Bubba Coskey and Foster Parker persuaded Headmaster John Cooper to bring Garry McMillan to Kinkaid. A highly successful coach at the Texas Military Institute, McMillan started his career at Kinkaid as a sixth grade history teacher and football coach. He had the opportunity later on to team-teach eighth grade U.S. history with Art Goddard, an experience he says that prepared him well for his move to teaching in Upper School. In 1978 McMillan was appointed Dean of Boys, a position he filled for many years in addition to his duties as history teacher and Head Coach of football. Having coached his teams to 16 Southwest Prepatory Conference titles in football, McMillan has served as a mentor to many young assistants who have gone on to coach rival teams in the SPC. In the winter and spring sports seasons over the years, McMillan has coached almost every sport, including several seasons of varsity girls' softball! He began the wrestling program at Kinkaid, and he continues to enjoy coaching the boys' golf and football teams as part of his duties as Director of Athletics.

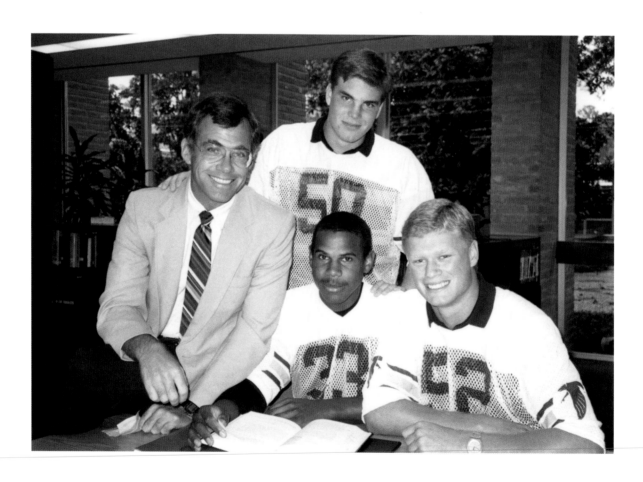

# J. Barry Moss

Barry Moss was a man of many parts: keeper of tradition, opponent of philosophical relativism, classroom innovator, wise counselor. He was the curmudgeon one most wanted to invite for dinner and the person one might like to see added to Mt. Rushmore.

Moss joined the faculty in 1960 as a recent graduate of Rice Institute and the Harvard Divinity School. Later on, a co-founder of Interim Term with Bill McKinley, he was Principal of Upper School for 17 years and Dean of Faculty for 16 years. Most importantly, Moss would say he remained a classroom teacher throughout all of his 44-year tenure at the School. He designed two of the most popular (and most challenging) courses at Kinkaid: the history of religion and the history of philosophy, which he taught in addition to classes in world literature. In 1986 he received the Columbiana Award for Excellence in Teaching, the only part-time faculty member ever to receive it.

Moss was a gifted administrator whose steady leadership in the sixties and seventies anchored parents and students during a time of many upheavals in education. His insistence on "consistent principles applied consistently" helped to keep Kinkaid's mission strong and clear.

Soon after Interim Term began, Moss introduced the opportunity for "academic travel" for Kinkaid students. His curiosity about how other people lived and what things were most important to them remained with him and with the students on those trips long after their Kinkaid days were over. The most important part of his life, Moss felt, was making a difference, contributing in a significant way, to Kinkaid. And that he did.

# Fred Northcutt and Linda Miller

Fred Northcutt and Linda Miller came to Kinkaid within one year of one another, in 1980 and 1981, respectively. The were hired by Headmaster Glenn Ballard to support his interest in strengthening the Science Department, and admirably they did just that.

Northcutt had been a leader of the Science Department at The Hockaday School in Dallas, and Miller, educated at the University of Chicago, had been a very successful teacher of advanced physics in Houston area public schools. Northcutt has taught physics, chemistry and astronomy, while Miller has continued to teach physics, as well as serving as Science Coordinator for Upper School.

As valuable as their contributions have been as members of the Kinkaid faculty, their service of almost 25 years as Coordinators of the Kinkaid-HISD Engineering Math Science Summer Institute has been even more outstanding. This program, which encourages primarily minority Upper School students from public schools to attend classes in math and science during the summer at Kinkaid, grew in prestige and support under the leadership of Miller and Northcutt. The program is the healthy, popular one it is today because they nurtured it, attracting superior teachers and enthusiastic students year after year.

# Thomas B. Peden

Tom Peden, who was once a "lifer" at St. John's School, has now been at Kinkaid much longer than the 13 years he spent cheering for the red and black. He came to our school in 1980, among the first teachers hired in Glenn Ballard's inaugural year as Headmaster. Peden holds degrees from the University of Texas and Princeton University. He has taught seventh and eighth grade English and served terms as Dean of both of those grades. In 2002 he added to his teaching duties an Upper School freshman English class, along with an Interim Term class in "American Military Power." His Interim Term class is a popular one for students who, like Peden, are interested in weaponry and especially combat airplanes. Much admired in the classroom for his love of literature and his teaching of good organizational skills, Peden was honored with the Columbiana Award for Excellence in Teaching in 1988.

Although he recently completed a term on the Alumni Board of St. John's, Peden's Kinkaid roots are strong. His father, David Peden, "graduated" as a member of Margaret Kinkaid's eighth grade class on the Elgin Street campus in 1923!

# Charles B. Sanders, Jr.

Charles B. Sanders, Jr. ('54), affectionately known as "Coach Charlie" to the multitude of students and faculty who have known him during his 40-plus years at the School, is a one-of-a-kind fan of Kinkaid. A graduate of the class of 1954, Sanders was a fine athlete, but when he wasn't on the field as a player, he was running the scoreboard and keeping stats on almost every boys' and girls' team in nearly every sport. He has been Kinkaid's official scorekeeper, sports statistics whiz and play-by-play announcer for home football games and Field Day for more years than anyone can remember. Fortunately for all of us, and particularly for the preparation of this book, he has been Kinkaid's archivist and collector of memorabilia for at least 45 years. Many of the photographs on these pages come from Sanders's fascinating office. He serves as Audio-Visual Director and seems to find a space for anything related to Kinkaid – from adobe tiles that once formed the roof of the Richmond Avenue school to the official Scrapbook of the Class of 2005.

Many people have wondered how Coach Charlie's devotion to Kinkaid began. He tells us that it began shortly after he arrived in Middle School, and it was sparked by Kinkaid's legendary coach Jack Hanagriff.

# GRADUATION MIRACLES

*I*n the 1940's the entire school attended Commencement. Teachers, whose daunting task was to keep energetic second and third graders quiet during the ceremony, have passed on an assortment of stories about how they managed. Some handed out "all day suckers" with the sticks removed. Some let a slow and steady stream of children slip in and out of the bathrooms. Some relied on hand-holding and threats.

In 1949 a heavy downpour threatened to ruin Commencement. Mrs. Kinkaid continued to organize students in spite of thunderclaps and drumming rain. Ten minutes before the opening music, the rain stopped. Henry Freeman, Kinkaid's beloved groundskeeper, ran out and dried the seats. Stunned students and parents proceeded with this miraculous Commencement precisely on time. One father was heard to say, "You know, I think Mrs. Kinkaid even tells God what to do!"

# SECOND CHANCES

*I* came to Kinkaid in kindergarten. By second grade, I still could not read even three-letter words, and I was absolutely hopeless at telling time. My rather exasperated teacher suggested to my parents that I might have had some type of learning problem and that I should perhaps attend a "special" school.

So it happened. I was placed in a "special" school, where we learned to put on our shoes and tie them for weeks on end. It was only by chance, some weeks later, that my father noticed I was unable to see a train properly. He took me to an ophthalmologist, who, lo and behold, discovered my sight was very poor. After I got my glasses, I was shocked to see that words were composed of individual letters, and time got much easier to tell when I discovered that those black smudges were actually numbers and that clocks had hands!

Mrs. Kinkaid called my mother to see how I was getting along in the new school, and my mother painted a rather dismal picture. The school was fine, but I was very unhappy there. "Bring Susan to see me tomorrow at three o'clock, please," Mrs. Kinkaid said.

At that meeting, Mrs. Kinkaid proffered milk and two sugar cookies. She spoke with me at some length, and then said, "I think you belong in this School, and I will be interested in your progress." Mrs. Kinkaid did not know about my poor eyesight. She simply decided to give me a second chance.

Kinkaid remains a place of second chances, where one's worth isn't judged by letters on a report card, but rather by one's potential and the quality of one's heart. In the eighth grade, Mr. Goddard asked our class what careers we might like to train for in college. When I said, "Teaching," he replied, "Be careful that you mean it, for teaching is not a job; it is a calling — and its requirements are very different from those praised in the business world. Its rewards, however, are much greater." Thanks to Mrs. Kinkaid, I had the chance to find out just how right Art Goddard was.

SUSAN HILLEBRANDT SANTANGELO, CLASS OF 1955

# Susan H. Santangelo

Susan Hillebrandt Santangelo ('55), a third-generation Houstonian and a "lifer" at Kinkaid, was a class officer, played three varsity sports, served as editor of *The Falcon* and graduated as valedictorian of her class. After graduating from Wellesley College, she returned to Houston where she obtained an M.A. in English and taught at both Texas Southern University and the University of Houston.

In 1976 Headmaster John Cooper persuaded Santangelo to come to Kinkaid as part-time teacher of journalism and assistant to College Counselor Mary Vaughan. Soon she was a member of the full-time staff and since that time has worn many hats: tennis coach, Dean of Girls, teacher of English, Director of Publications and at present Dean of Students. During the 1980-1981 school year, she researched and wrote *Kinkaid and Houston: 75 Years*, a detailed account of the School's beginning. She is proud to be one of the two current staff members (the other is Charlie Sanders) who were once students on the Richmond Avenue campus under Margaret Kinkaid.

When Phyllis Selber came to Kinkaid in 1979 from Shreveport, her original position was in the Admissions Office. A year later she was asked to join the Development Office. Immediately, Selber realized that the School was almost 75 years old and did not have an Alumni Office. Besides a desk and a file cabinet, she found no alumni records, no formal organizational structure for alumni and no plan to start one! Selber changed all that.

She suggested that the Alumni and Business offices should be separated as they were in other independent schools. Later, as Development Director, she oversaw the creation of our current Alumni Association which grew out of the Alumni Phonathon that Selber started in 1983 as a way to "get back in touch" with Kinkaid's vast numbers of alumni.

Selber is fond of calling ALL of the School's alumni, "my alums." One might say that much of the success of the recent capital campaign is due, in fact, to the relationship building that the Development and Alumni Offices main-tained during her 23 years at Kinkaid.

When Selber retired in 2001, the Development Office had witnessed the construction of a new Lower School building, a new theatre and the Center for Student Life, Fine Arts and Administration. Building on a solid foun-dation, the Development and Alumni Offices have many new projects under way and alumni activities are burgeoning

## Harriett and Zahari "Zack" Semander

Zack Semander came to Kinkaid in 1966 because John Cooper had heard that he was an especially outstanding teacher of math who could teach "on any level to any kind of student." Born in Greece, Semander was fluent in math on two continents. He served as Chairman of the Math Department and as Kinkaid's golf coach for many years. The annual Zack Semander Alumni Golf Tournament is named in his honor.

In 1973 Semander's wife, Harriett, became part of the office staff. Her professionalism and organizational skills were legendary in Middle School where her nursing skills were often required throughout her early years when Kinkaid had no "official" nurse. All of the Semanders' children graduated from Kinkaid. The tragic murder of their eldest daughter, Elena, by serial killer Coral Eugene Watts in 1982 sparked Harriett, with her husband's full support, to initiate a campaign to keep Watts in prison for life and to support the rights of victims and their families nationwide.

Twenty years after Elena's death, when Watts was about to be released from prison on a technicality, Harriett organized an anniversary memorial service at her church that was attended by the families of Watts's victims from all over the country. As a result of that effort, a witness came forward whose testimony ensured that Watts would spend the rest of his life in prison.

In 2005 Harriett Semander received the Leon Goldstein Crime Stoppers Award, given to a citizen who has made a significant contribution to fighting crime and making our community a safer place in which to live.

# Louise Shreckengaust

Louise Donlon, recently divorced, came to Kinkaid from New England to teach history in 1946. She met and married Quincy Shreckengaust one summer a few years later. Mrs. Kinkaid, saying that Shreckengaust was too much of a mouthful for students (and perhaps not saying that she was reluctant to admit that a remarried divorcée was teaching at her school) asked Louise to continue to teach under the name "Donlon." So Mrs. Donlon it was, until one exam time when she invited her students to come to her home for a study session before the test. The students noticed a strange man's name on the mailbox and concluded, correctly, that Mrs. Donlon was living with a man! The scandalous news spread like wildfire over the weekend, and by Monday morning, Mrs. Kinkaid, not a little embarrassed, told the Upper School students that they would just have to learn to say and spell Shreckengaust, for that was "Mrs. Donlon's" proper name! Shreckengaust was immediately shortened to "Shreck," and both Mr. and Mrs. Shreck became fixtures at sports events and performances for many years afterwards.

Louise Shreckengaust was a fine teacher of history, but she was even more gifted at motivating young people. "I think you can do it – why not try?" was what she said to discouraged students, and they did try, and most of the time they succeeded. "Mrs. Shreck gave me the confidence to be smart," one Yale graduate said.

# Mary Vaughan

Mary Vaughan was part of Kinkaid's Upper School for 27 years. She served simultaneously in two demanding capacities: Dean of Girls and Director of College Guidance. When she began her tenure under John Cooper, "college guidance" was in its infancy. Vaughan researched information on colleges, visited in the summers and sometimes during the school year, and began to establish the fine relationships Kinkaid enjoys today with institutions around the country. She wrote college recommendations for every senior and helped each one complete his or her applications.

Additionally, in her position as Dean of Girls, she handled advising, discipline and course selections for many students. She was the "guru of graduation" as well, and as such oversaw Commencement and all its related activities.

How did she do it all? "Very well!" is the resounding answer generations of graduates would agree.

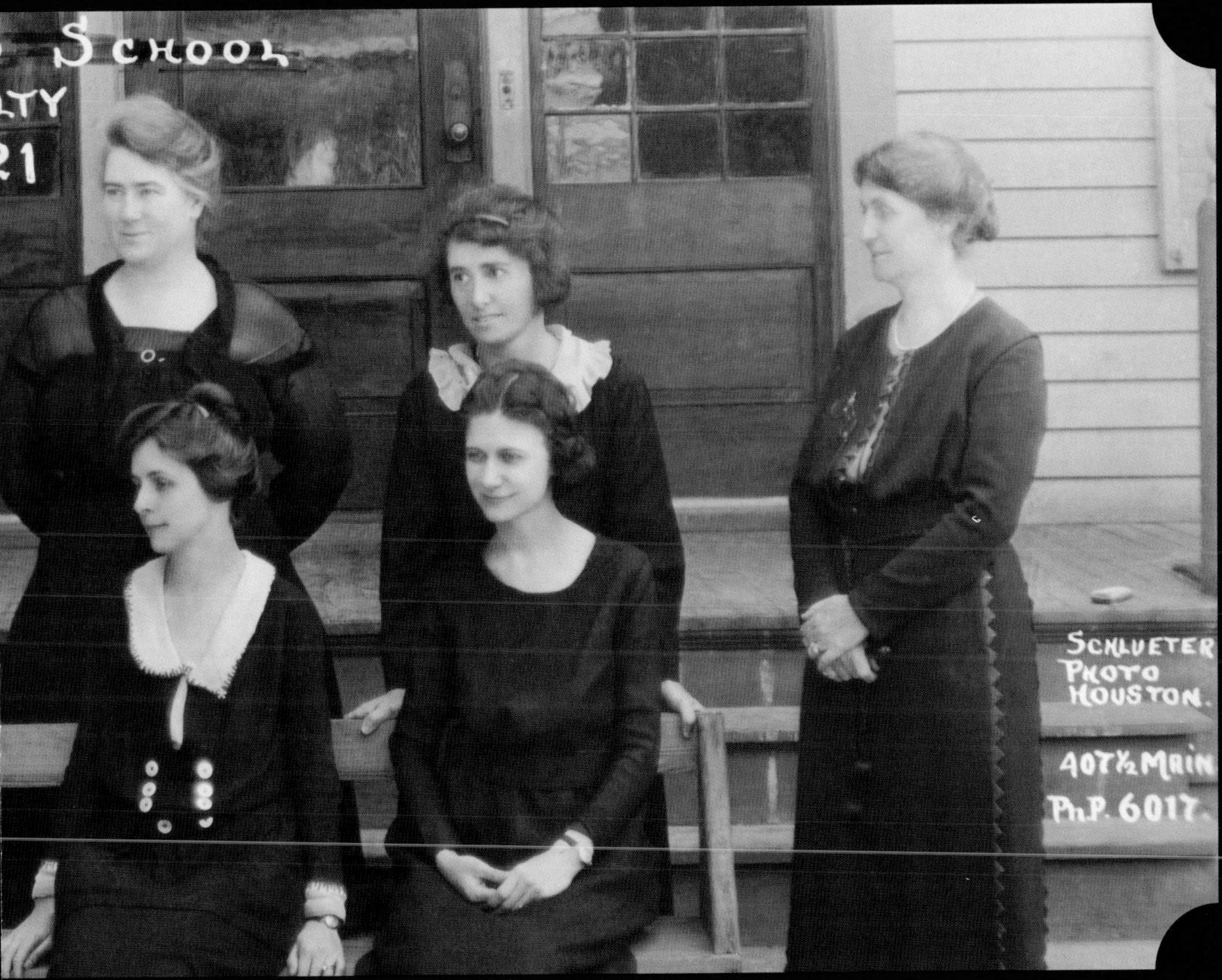
SCHOOL
LTY
21
SCHLUETER
PHOTO
HOUSTON.
407½ MAIN
Ph.P. 6017.

# Deborah and David Veselka

David Veselka's coming to Kinkaid was serendipitous. Mary Vaughan, who was Dean of Girls at the time, met Veselka, who had been teaching in high school in Fort Bend County, when they had jury duty together. She persuaded him to apply for a job at Kinkaid, and although he was leery at first of accepting a Middle School position, he signed on to teach seventh grade history and eighth grade English at Kinkaid in 1978.

Veselka's interest and expertise in photography, along with his enjoyment of Upper School students, led him to offer Kinkaid's first class in photography. These classes became so sought after by students that in 1996 he relinquished his position as Middle School English teacher and concentrated all his time on photography. Still he has to turn students away for lack of space! That his students have won the top prize in the Texas State Photography Competition for four out of the last six years underscores the expertise and creativity of his teaching.

In 1980 Deborah Veselka was a very successful teacher of science in HISD when Kinkaid had an opening in middle school science. She decided to join David, and in that first year, she taught both algebra and physical science to eighth graders. In recent years her leadership as Chair of the Science Department has fostered excellent cooperation between Middle and Upper School science faculties and has made the Science Department one of the strongest at Kinkaid.

Deborah and David Veselka have served in Middle School for a combined 54 years. Both of them have been winners of the Columbiana Award for Excellence in Teaching. The Veselkas have seen many of their students go on to careers in the sciences or in photography, but perhaps they are most gratified when they hear that a non-scientist has learned to appreciate ecology, or a student who didn't know an F-stop from a stop sign delights in taking artistic photographs.

# Leigh Weld

A current parent, who is also an alum, said recently that he thought Leigh Weld knew more about Kinkaid than almost anyone. He may be correct, for during Weld's 29 years at the School, he had many duties. John Cooper hired him to teach math in the Middle School but he soon added coaching to his duties. When activities of the Mothers' Club became numerous, Mr. Weld was the person called on to act as liaison. Later on, he helped with cafeteria operations, facilities management and finally became assistant to both Art Goddard and John Cooper.

No job was too big or too small for Weld to handle with aplomb. He was unflappable and always a gentleman regardless of the "crisis" at hand. On more than one occasion, mothers in charge of Field Day counted on his help to get booths up at the last minute or even to cook hot dogs if that was what was needed.

In the classroom, Mr. Weld was patient and made even the poorest math student feel comfortable. As a result, his students wanted to please him, and many surprised themselves by doing much better in this class than they had anticipated. As Mr. Goddard's right-hand man, Weld was responsible for a good number of disciplinary matters over the years, and he handled them so calmly and fairly that the students involved, as well as their parents, admired him.

Weld retired in 1981 after 29 years of service to Kinkaid.

# Tom Wey

Tom Wey came to Kinkaid in 1976 as a math teacher and coach of JV football as well as varsity baseball and track. Over the years he has undertaken many responsibilities, among them Dean of Boys. Today he is the defensive coordinator for our varsity football team, the Director of Interim Term and the person who schedules classes for all Upper School students.

Wey has led Interim Term trips to China five times. His interest in that country and its people has led to an appreciation of Chinese art and at least one semester of studying Mandarin at Rice University. Wey's office is the busiest place in the Upper School at the start of each semester as students seek his expertise in fine-tuning their schedules. Amid the hubbub he remains calm and focused, and more often than not, he finds solutions to their scheduling problems.

When he is not on the playing field, in the classroom or at his computer, Wey likes to be in less "civilized" surroundings where he can enjoy the woods or the water and spend some time hunting and fishing.

ATHLETICS

# Sam Windsor

In 1950 Mrs. Kinkaid employed Sam Windsor to teach math in Middle School. During his 38 years at the School, he taught math in both Middle and Upper Schools, coached various sports and served as chaperon on countless school trips. Mrs. Kinkaid admired his calm demeanor in the face of almost any student antic, and Windsor admits today that there is very little in the way of student behavior that he hasn't witnessed. His colleagues found in Windsor a quiet strength that echoed his support of the School and his willingness to be of service to them as well as his students.

Many a parent who despaired of his or her child's ever succumbing to the discipline of math has benefited from Windsor's experience and reassurance, and many students whose favorite subject was definitely not math have benefited from his patience and his willingness to persevere with them. "What we all felt was that whether we were A students or not, Mr. Windsor still liked us and would still come out to see us play or sing or act," an admiring student said. Windsor retired from teaching in 1988, but he is a familiar face on campus as he attends games and performances and reunions at the School. His legacy of loyalty and interest in everything Kinkaidian continues.

# The Future

Was it Shakespeare who wrote: "The past is but prologue to the future"? In this wonderful book, you have read about Kinkaid's past and about many of the impressive people who have shaped or been shaped by this remarkable School. Kinkaid's collective culture, built and maintained lovingly by so many, enriches the lives of all who work and learn here today.

But as impressive as the first 100 years have been, the future holds great promise and excitement for Kinkaid, and I am absolutely certain that the best is yet to come!

The world in which our graduates will live and work will be different from the world of today. Both the challenges that they will face and their opportunity to make a difference in that world will be breathtaking.

Information technology will completely flatten the barriers of geography. Business, education, science, medicine, public service and so many other endeavors will be increasingly global. Leaders in this world will need, among other things, the following: skills, knowledge and confidence with information technology; understanding and appreciation for different cultures, races, languages and religions; the ability and readiness to generate, innovate, think strategically and learn; understanding of, and commitment to, excellence; and perhaps most important, a clear moral compass.

Kinkaid educates leaders. Through its curriculum, athletics and arts programs, student government, extracurricular activities, opportunities for travel and for community service, and emphasis on character development, Kinkaid will prepare its graduates not only to flourish, but also to lead in the world they will enter as adults.

Thank you for your interest in, and support of, this special School. With you I look forward to a great future for Kinkaid! ▪

Don North, Headmaster

# AN ANNUAL TREAT

*A* favorite tradition is the long anticipated visit of the prekindergarten and kindergarten children to "trick or treat" in offices and classrooms throughout the School.

On the first Halloween of Don North's tenure, he dressed in a Dracula costume and stood in my office and greeted children. The following year, I asked if I could decorate his office, which I did – very simply the first year – and now I decorate the conference room, too.

One year I decorated his office like a graveyard – complete with a big mural of a haunted house drawn in glow-in-the-dark paint. I put green outdoor carpet on the floor and had several "grave markers" that lit up. I scattered plastic glow-in-the-dark bones on the floor.

Don had a full-body skeleton suit with bones on the front that also glowed in the dark. He was seated next to one of the grave markers in a chair covered in black, and since the room was dark (with only a black light), all you saw was a skeleton sitting down. When all the kids got into the room, Don stood up and started talking in a very deep voice – and you can guess what happened – lots of screaming.

But the best part was later, after Don went to class. Children would come back through the building after visiting the Upper School. My door was open and so was Don's; they could see the graveyard, and they asked if they could look at it with the light on. They all asked where the skeleton was and I told them I didn't know. He just disappeared. One small child, waving a plastic bone in each hand, yelled, "I know what happened! He just fell apart. Here are his bones!"

**JEANIE BINNS, ASSISTANT TO THE HEADMASTER**

*For 25 years Jeanie has served Glenn Ballard and Don North in a myriad of administrative matters.*

# AN ENDURING MISTAKE

*W*hen Kinkaid opened the Richmond Avenue campus in the 1920's, the first Alumni
Association presented Mrs. Kinkaid with a bronze plaque incorrectly commemorating
the founding year of the School as 1906. The School had actually started in 1904 in her cottage on
Elgin Street and San Jacinto Street. Mrs. Kinkaid showed no dismay. She graciously accepted the
plaque from the Association President, actress Virgilia Chew. From then on, 1906 was recognized,
albeit incorrectly, as the founding of Kinkaid.

# SPECIAL ACKNOWLEDGMENTS

## KINKAID CENTENNIAL BOOK COMMITTEE

**Chairmen**

Roni Obermayer Atnipp
Elizabeth Jacobs Labanowski ('73)
Susan Hillebrandt Santangelo ('55)
Susan Savage Thompson

**Faculty / Staff Advisors**

Tom Moore, Development
Lynn Meyer Fort ('68), Alumni
Jennifer Pardee, Centennial
Charles B. Sanders, Jr. ('54), Archives

**Decade Chairmen**

1906-1939
Martha Lartigue
Dinnie Smith Mowery ('36)
Kathy Sangalis
Annie Ray Watkin Strange ('30)

1940-1949
Pam Lovett
Francita Stuart Koelsch Ulmer ('49)
Caro Ivy Walker ('46)

1950-1959
Lucy Lee Lamme ('58)

1960-1969
Lana Lee Cureton ('63)
Susie Adams Smith ('69)

1970-1979
Melissa Lyon Johnson ('74)
Karen Abramson Selzer ('82)

1980-1989
Karen Hankamer Horne ('88)

1990-1999
Kate Lovett Searls ('93)

**Research Committee**

Courtnay Tartt Elias ('84), Coordinator
Julie Brown
Alison Chambers
Betsy Nettles
Karen Wilkinson

**History / Timeline Committee**

Ruth Ereli
Patti Morgan
Giggy Martin Thanheiser ('77)
Anne Thomson

**Anecdotes**

Peggy Rathmell

**Photography Committee**

Betsy Haas - Advisor
Charlotte Orr
Kim Wind

**Marketing / Communications Committee**

Judy Lee
Shelley MacKay
Gwen Smith

**Book Orders**

Catherine Choate Christopherson ('75)
Laura Griffin Schuhmacher ('82)

**Nominations Records Coordinator**

Estelle Racusin

---

## CENTENNIAL STEERING COMMITTEE

**Headmaster**

Donald C. North

**Chairmen**

Emily Attwell Crosswell ('59)
O. Holcombe Crosswell ('58)

**Board of Trustees Representative**

Frances Hopper Jeter ('74)
Walter G. Mayfield ('81)

**Alumni Board Presidents**

Milton H. West III ('71)
2004-2005

Clare Crosswell McLeroy ('88)
2005-2006

**Student Representatives**

Sarah Hogarty ('06)
Stephen Viviano ('06)

**Parents of Alumni Representatives**

Nancy and Jim Gordon

**Grandparents Representatives**

Isla and T.R. Reckling

**Presidents of Parents Association**

Anne Coskey and Carol Herder
2004-2005

Ann Bookout and Robin Floyd
2005-2006

**Centennial Book Co-Chairs**

Roni Atnipp
Elizabeth Jacobs Labanowski ('73)
Susan Hillebrandt Santangelo ('55)
Susan Thompson

**Centennial Advisor**

Phyllis Selber

**Alumni Advisor**

Lynn Meyer Fort ('68)

**Faculty Representative**

Susan Hillebrandt Santangelo ('55)

**Director of Development**

Tom Moore

**Ex-officio Historian**

Charles B. Sanders, Jr. ('54)

**Centennial Liaison**

Jennifer Pardee

## CENTENNIAL HOST COMMITTEE

Dan Arnold ('47)
Jennifer Tuttle Arnold ('78)
Doug Aron ('92)
Myron G. Blalock III ('72)
Dunbar Chambers, Jr. ('53)
Jay B. Coskey ('76)
Lana Lee Cureton ('63)
Linda Beeley Denison ('58)
Brad Deutser ('83)
Jill Lichtenstein Deutser ('89)
Tami Baird Dyer ('58)
Canaan Factor ('96)
Ed H. Frank III ('68)
Jane Heyck Gaucher ('53)
John David Hagerman ('59)
Katherine Susman Howe ('64)
Webb Jennings ('89)
Elyse Spector Kalmans ('87)
Stephen Lasher ('66)
Mary Nell Jeffers Lovett ('63)
Joan E. Herrin Lyons ('47)
Katie Medlen ('95)
Christine Robertson Morenz ('92)
Ashley Morgan ('93)
Sarah Wheless Murrin ('90)
Bob Phillips ('62)
Betsy Bowen Phillips ('63)
Jil Robins Pollock

Steve Retzloff ('74)
Meredith Riddle ('95)
Adrian Turner Ross ('62)
Kate Lovett Searls ('93)
Madeleine Topper Sheehy ('74)
Susie Adams Smith ('69)
Leslie Sprague
Robert L. Stanton ('89)
Lisa Crosswell Stone ('83)
Douglas E. Swanson, Jr. ('90)
Courtney Marinis Swanson ('91)
Matt Thanheiser ('76)
Francita Stuart Koelsch Ulmer ('49)
David M. Underwood ('54)
J. Malcolm Waddell ('70)

**Parents of Alumni**

Polly and Murry Bowden
Barbara and Bob Collie
Nancy and Jack Dinerstein
Cindy and Don Poarch
Cindy and Ron Soefer

**Grandparents**

Janie and Dick Beeler
President and Mrs. George H. W. Bush
Marilyn and Reb Gregg
Chris and Don Sanders

---

## THE FOUNDING BOARD OF TRUSTEES OF THE KINKAID SCHOOL

Burke Baker
R. L. Blaffer
W. L. Clayton
E. L. Neville
H. C. Wiess

## CHAIRMEN OF THE BOARD OF TRUSTEES

| | |
|---|---|
| 1924-1942 | Robert L. Blaffer |
| 1943-1947 | James A. Baker, Jr. |
| 1947-1949 | Milton E. Underwood |
| 1948-1953 | Isaac Arnold |
| 1953-1954 | Dunbar Chambers |
| 1954-1955 | W. J. Goldston |
| 1955-1957 | J. W. Hershey |
| 1957-1958 | L. Daffan Gilmer |
| 1958-1961 | W. Stewart Boyle |
| 1961-1963 | Foster Parker |
| 1963-1966 | Paul Taft |

| | |
|---|---|
| 1966-1968 | W. Buck Arnold |
| 1968-1970 | Robert Mosbacher |
| 1970-1972 | Paul F. Barnhart |
| 1972-1974 | J. Hugh Liedtke |
| 1974-1976 | Max R. Lents |
| 1977-1979 | Bruce Anderson |
| 1979-1981 | William Randolph Smith |
| 1981-1983 | O. Holcombe Crosswell ('58) |
| 1983-1985 | David M. Underwood ('54) |

| | |
|---|---|
| 1985-1987 | Randall Meyer |
| 1987-1989 | Ernest Deal |
| 1989-1991 | W. M. Wheless III |
| 1991-1993 | Jack H. Mayfield, Jr. |
| 1993-1995 | Stewart Cureton, Jr. |
| 1995-1999 | Mary Nell Jeffers Lovett ('63) |
| 1999-2002 | Stuart Yudofsky |
| 2002-2005 | John B. Beckworth |
| 2005-2008 | Frances Hopper Jeter ('74) |

# SPECIAL ACKNOWLEDGMENTS

## DISTINGUISHED ALUMNI AWARD RECIPIENTS 1991-2005

### 1991
Honorary Distinguished Alumnus
John H. Cooper

Distinguished Alumna
Laura Lee Scurlock Blanton ('46)

Distinguished Young Alumnus
Jeff Martin ('78)

### 1992
Honorary Distinguished Alumnus
William S. Kilroy

Distinguished Alumnus
David M. Underwood ('54)

Distinguished Young Alumnus
Clark Kent Ervin ('77)

### 1993
Honorary Distinguished Alumnus
Arthur E. Goddard

Distinguished Alumna
Wilhelmina Cullen Robertson ('40)

Distinguished Young Alumna
Kelly Sweeney McShane ('83)

### 1994
Honorary Distinguished Alumnus
Paul F. Barnhart, Sr.

Distinguished Alumnus
Damon Wells, Jr. ('54)

Distinguished Young Alumnus
Thomas G. Dunlap ('80)

### 1995
Honorary Distinguished Alumna
G'Ann Boyd

Distinguished Alumni
Emily Attwell Crosswell ('59)
O. Holcombe Crosswell ('58)

Distinguished Young Alumnus
Robert T. Baldwin ('77)

### 1996
Honorary Distinguished Alumnus
Max Lents

Distinguished Alumnus
William P. Hobby, Jr. ('49)

Distinguished Young Alumnus
Vernon Scott ('79)

### 1997
Honorary Distinguished Alumnus
J. Barry Moss

Distinguished Alumnus
A. J. Carothers ('50)

Distinguished Young Alumna
Vianei Lopez Robinson ('85)

### 1998
Honorary Distinguished Alumnus
Randall Meyer

Distinguished Alumna
Wilhelmina (Beth) Robertson ('64)

Distinguished Young Alumna
Lisa Brannon-Peppas ('80)

### 1999
Honorary Distinguished Alumna
Celina Kilpatrick

Distinguished Alumna
Mary Nell Jeffers Lovett ('63)

Distinguished Young Alumnus
Philip Stephenson ('83)

### 2000
Alumnae who attended school
in Mrs. Kinkaid's House

Katharine Parker Gregg Belton ('30)
Betty Ann Dionne Brannon ('27)
George Anna Lucas Burke ('28)
Rosalie Sherman Cartwright ('27)
Mary Frances Bowles Couper ('28)
Julia Vinson Dabney ('28)
Lida Arnold Edmundson ('28)
Carolyn Grant Fay ('29)
Burdine Clayton Johnson ('26)
Flora Streetman Lawhon ('21)
Alice Baker Jones Meyers ('31)
Jane Blaffer Owen ('30)
Alice Evans Pratt ('30)
Mary Jane Hale Rommel ('31)
Lucille Meachum Rutledge ('32)
Ann Ray Watkin Strange ('30)
Virginia Dunn Whitley ('30)
Ellen Hamilton Wilkerson ('22)

### 2001
Honorary Distinguished Alumnus
Jack H. Mayfield, Jr.

Distinguished Alumnus
Thomas D. Barrow ('41)

Distinguished Young Alumnus
Brian VanDeMark ('78)

### 2002
Honorary Distinguished Alumna
Phyllis Selber

Distinguished Alumnus
Daniel C. Arnold ('47)

Distinguished Young Alumnus
Johnny K. Sutton ('79)

### 2003
Honorary Distinguished Alumnus
John J. Germann

Distinguished Alumnus
Marc J. Shapiro ('65)

Distinguished Young Alumnus
Temple W. Williams III ('83)

### 2004
Honorary Distinguished Alumnus
J. B. "Bubba" Coskey

Distinguished Alumna
Frances Hopper Jeter ('74)

Distinguished Young Alumnus
C. Park Shaper ('86)

### 2005
Honorary Distinguished Alumnus
David M. Weekley

Distinguished Alumna
Francita Stuart Koelsch Ulmer ('49)

Distinguished Alumnus
Charles B. Sanders, Jr. ('54)

Distinguished Alumna
Susan Hillebrandt Santangelo ('55)

Distinguished Young Alumnus
Charles (Chuck) L. Scofield ('88)

# UNDERWRITERS

**THE KINKAID SCHOOL CENTENNIAL CELEBRATION ACKNOWLEDGES WITH GREAT APPRECIATION THE GENEROSITY OF THE FOLLOWING UNDERWRITERS:***

## PREMIER UNDERWRITERS ($25,000)

Janie and Dick Beeler

Debra and Dan Friedkin

Ruth and Jack Gay

Susan and Jack Mayfield

C. N. and Maria Papadopoulos
Charitable Foundation

Chris and Don Sanders

Bonnie and David Weekley

## FOUNDERS ($10,000)

Anonymous

Terri Lacy and James V. Baird

Mr. and Mrs. George Ball / William R.
Brown III / Ben Sewell Brown

Mr. and Mrs. A. L. Ballard

Janice and Tom Barrow

Polly and Murry Bowden

Nanette and Jerry Finger

Diane and Graham Gilliam

Lisa and Michael Holthouse

Mr. and Mrs. Bradley N. Howell

Lucy and Michael Kuhn / Bracewell
and Giuliani LLP

Mr. and Mrs. Hugh E. McGee III

Mr. and Mrs. Frank B. McGuyer

Barbara and Randall Meyer Family

The Chrissi and Mike Morgan Family

Isla and Tommy Reckling

Melissa and Doug Schnitzer

Mary Eliza and Park Shaper

Leslie and Abbott Sprague

Judy and Charles Tate

## BENEFACTORS ($5,000)

The E. Rudge Allen Family

Michelle and Lorne Bain

Mr. and Mrs. Myron G. Blalock III

Yvonne and L. P. Byler

Ellen and Jim Cummins Family

Ray C. Fish Foundation

Nancy and Jack Dinerstein

Mr. and Mrs. John W. Elias

Nancy and James Gordon

Reuven Hollo

Mr. and Mrs. Peter K. Jameson

Lara and Phillip Ladin / Jean and Ronnie Ladin

Mimi and Todd Marix

Sheila and Tad Mayfield

Flo and Bill McGee

Suzette and Walter Negley

Don, Cindy, Caroline and Allison Poarch

Barbara and Corbin J. Robertson, Jr.

Susan Hillebrandt Santangelo
and Sam Santangelo

The Tower Family

The Diana and Conrad Weil, Jr. Family Fund

## SPONSORS ($2,500)

Jennifer Tuttle Arnold and Steven Arnold

Beverly and Dan Arnold

Trisha and Edward Baird

Carin and Todd Barth

Ann and John Bookout

Galeen and J. Mark Breeding

Nancy and Harry Burrow

Trish and Dunbar Chambers

Barbara and Bob Collie

Sarah and Sam Cooper

Emily and Holcombe Crosswell

Mary and Stephen Dyer

Tami and Pat Dyer

Ellen, Tommy and Elizabeth Ford

Dr. Allen Gaw and Dr. Betty Lee

Jennifer and Lance Gilliam

Susie and Jay Golding, Jarrett,
Stephen and Kyle Golding

Christa and Vince Hash

Tinta and Pablo Henning

Carol and Charlie Herder

Pam and Alan Jarrett

Frances and Rick Jeter, Emily Catherine
and Tany Jeter

Laura L. and J. Chris Jones

Debbie and Jeff Karchmer

Barbara and Charles Kraft

Hon. and Mrs. Sim Lake

Judy and Frank Lee - Grace, Parker,
Perry and Jay

Mary Nell and Malcolm Lovett

Mr. and Mrs. William R. Lloyd, Jr.

Joan H. Lyons

Barbara Lister, M.D. and Daniel E. McCormick

The Mead Family – Gary, Janet and Kimberly

Patti and Michael Morgan

Dr. Bruce and Denise Moseley

Beverly and Staman Ogilvie

Anne Owen and Harold Pontez

Ann and Hugh Roff

The Rogers Family – Rex, Diane,
Anna and Christina

Lee and Gary Rosenthal

Linda and Alan Rosen

Amy and Peter Shaper

Jeri and Marc Shapiro

Ginny and L. E. Simmons

Mr. and Mrs. Frank C. Smith, Jr.

The Tilney Family

Mr. and Mrs. James G. Ulmer

Leslye and David Weaver

Barbara and Temple Webber

Jane Edmond and Randal Weber

Mr. and Mrs. R. Graham Whaling

Mr. and Mrs. Bert Winston, Jr.

Mr. and Mrs. Madison Woodward III

## FALCON FANS ($500)

The Altman Family - Larry, Ann Marie, Laura and Megan

The Atnipp Family - Roni, Doug, Julia, Sarah, Ben and Will

Skyler, Kendall and Kate Bentsen

The Bernell Family - Ron, Carolyn, Brent and Katie

The Brener - Hellmund Family - Alfredo, Celina, Leon and Nina

Dr. Fred J. Bressler and Family

The Clawater Family - Jean Rose, Grace, Hollee and Wayne

The Coskeys - Anne, Jay, Julia and Andrew

Paige and Chelsea Cunningham

Ernest Deal

Robert, Nathaniel and Carson Finger

The Foulard Family - Georgia, Mike, George and Lilly

Mr. and Mrs. Earl Hankamer and Family

Claire Schlumberger Henry

The Hopper Family - John, Sally, Ginny and Eliza

Lee and Joe Jamail

Jim, Karen, Scot, Shelley and Stephanie Johnson

Jeanie Kilroy

The Labanowski Family - Paul, Elizabeth, John, Lawrence, Charles, William, Gregory and Mary

Edward A. and Anne T. Lasater

Paige and Charlie Nettles

Dan, Reiko, Elaine and Emily Nip

Mary and Don North

The Pinchal Family

Eliza Lovett Randall

Carroll Robertson Ray

Hugh and Ann Roff

The Scofield Family - John, Denise, Ellen, Mary Caroline and Jack

The Sheffield Family - Don, Nancy, Ward, Laura, Ward, Jr. and Davis

Samuel and Roberta Smiley

The James Thompson Family - Jim, Susan, Lauren and Parker

David and Lynda Underwood

The John S. Ivy Family - 14 Kinkaid Alumni

The Wang Family - Jen, Yai-li, May and Iris

The Wilder Foundation - Rita Johnson Wilder

The Wilson Family - Welcome, Jr. and Anita, Christina, Courtney, Kelly, Anna Catherine and Welcome III

Dr. and Mrs. Robert S. Zeller and Family

## CHEERLEADERS ($250)

Sue Sue and Don Aron

Emma Thurmond and Family

Lynne Bentsen

Milton and Bess Black

The Chavez Family - Daniel, Marigel, Daniel and Karla

The Crosswell Family - Holcombe, Ligon, Emily, Will, Greyson, Mary Grey, Henry

The Detering Faimly - Kit, Carl, Cassie and Carlos III

The Farris Family - George, Madelyn, Leigh, Lindsay and Bobby

The Fernández Family - Randy, Emilia, Javier and Chantal

Mr. and Mrs. Robert E. Fondren

Dr. and Mrs. Michael Fordis

Cullen K. Geiselman

Mr. and Mrs. Charles R. Gregg and Family

The Harper Family - John II; Cynthia; John III and Leslie

Sally and David Harvin, Kimberly, Billy and John

The Herder Family - Charlie, Carol, Sarah and Charles

George and Katherine Howe

The Johnson Family - Mark, Pat, Matthew and Phillip

Mr. and Mrs. Todd Johnson and Family

The Kirkwood Family - Andrew, Martha, Matthew and Talley

The Kirshon Family - Brian, Carol, Layne and Samantha

Barbara and Charles Kraft

Mr. and Mrs. Larry Levine and Family

Mr. and Mrs. Mark Levine and Family

Pamela and Edgar O. Lovett

Maria and Christopher Pappas, James, Katina, Georgea, Victoria and Michael

The Rathmell Family - John, Peggy, Mary Katherine, John and Laura

Beth Robertson, Grover Geiselman and Cullen Geiselman

Charles B. Sanders, Jr.

The Selber Family - Phyllis, Jack, Jill and Sandy

Bob and Patsy Speed

The Stukalin Family - David, Elizabeth and Sarah

The Sellers Thomas Family

Mr. and Mrs. Joseph W. Thomson III and Family

Emma Thurmond and Family

Frances Fondren and Robert C. Wilson III Family - Jennifer W. Brown, Melanie W. Bates, Carson Wilson, Michael Hanson, Burton Hanson and Anah Marie Hanson

Dr. and Mrs. William L. Winters, Jr. and Family

Lyn and John Woodhouse

The Yudofsky Family - Stuart, Beth, Elissa, Lynn and Emily

## VARSITY ($100)

The John Adkins Family / Richard and Alice Colvin

The Alexander Family - Audrey, Lane, Leslie, Steven, Caroline and Andy

Carol C. Allbritton

Dr. and Mrs. James E. Allison III

Hon. and Mrs. John Sharp Anderson

The Anderson Family - Kent, Linda, Whitney, Huntley and Clarke

Mr. and Mrs. Scott Anderson and Family

The Arcidiacono Family - James, Kathy, Jamie, Andrew, Will and Emily

Beverly and Dan Arnold

The Arnold Family - Elizabeth, Robbie, Ella Rose and Ruby

Mr. and Mrs. Doug Aron

The Baerenstecher Family - John, Karen, Halle and Julia

The Baker Family - Georgia, Chip and Lovett

The Banos Family - George, Becky, George, John and Jane

The Barrere Family - Jamie, Clem and John

The Barth Family - Todd, Carin, Mitchell, Leslye and Melysa

Kay Read Bartle

The Bay Family - Thomas, Sarah, Melissa and James

Bill and Nancy Baycroft

The Rick Beeler Family

Michaela, Joe, Tommy and Cassie Beeler

The Bell Family - René, Terry and Charles

(Continued on next page)

# UNDERWRITERS

## VARSITY ($100) CONTINUED

Rhoda and Stuart Benson

The Berman Family - Phil, Elly,
Jeffrey and Kevin

Melisa Lynn Billingsley

Jeanie and Billy Binns

The Blalock Family - Myron,
Rosanna, Geer and Holly

William S. Blomdahl

Susan and Michael Bono

The Bookout Family - John, Ann,
John, James and Katherine

The Botts Family - Gerald, Sue,
Thomas and Katherine

The Bramel Family

The Brass Family - Katie, A.J.,
Hallie and Joycie

Ms. Dana M. Brown

The Brown Family - Deborah,
Barrett and Audrey

The Brown Family - Zachry, Aline,
Andrea, Carter, Sarah and Marie

Chip, Sharon and Charlie Bryan

Nancy Burch and Family

The Burke Family - Walter, Dana,
Caroline, Thomas and Walter

Mr. and Mrs. Cliff W. Burrow and Family

Nancy and Harry Burrow and Family

The Cain Family - Walker, Marjorie,
Sara and Walker

Ellie and Roy Camberg - Bradley,
Adelaide and Will Beard

Carlton Carl

The Carl Family - Lucy, William, Noble,
Anne, Elizabeth and Virginia

Mrs. Jack H. Castle, Sr.

Andrew, David and Clayton Chambers

Dunbar N. Chambers III and Joanna Gol

Dave and Erminie Chambers Chapman

Sarah E. Chapoton

The Christopherson Family - Walter,
Catherine, Emma and Will

The Cochran Family - Frost, Lisa,
Kelly, Shelley and William

Steve and Betty Cochran

The Cohen Family - Steven, Debra,
Courtney and Hilary

Mr. and Mrs. William Conner and Family

Mr. and Mrs. W. Loch Cook and Family

The Crawford Family - Marshall, Marjorie,
Marshall III, Mary Rodman and Cameron

Rosslyn and Marshall Crawford

Mr. and Mrs. D. Miller Crosswell, Jr.

The Crosswell Family - David, Carolyn,
Courtland, Miller and Allison

Chris and Sallie Cruger

The Cunningham Family - Scott,
Angelique and Katherine

The Currie Family - Peter, Lisa,
Mitchell and Jordan

Jimmy, Montana and Cheyenne Dawley

Mr. and Mrs. Matthew C. Deal and Family

The DeArman Family - Bill, Carol,
Nicholas and Alex

Todd and Laura Decker

The Decker Family - Liz, Bill, Katie and Will

Thomas Deskin

The Deutser Family - Brad, Jill,
Ashley and Andrew

John and Martha Diffey

Joan and Steve Dinerstein, Jeff and Mark

The Dinerstein Family - Nancy and Jack,
Brian and Liz, Ross and Brad

Mr. and Mrs. Andrew Scott Dixon and Family

Bob, Katherine and Katie Dowdell

Doug and Sheryl Doyle

The Emerson Family - Eric, Jennifer and Ayden

The Ereli Family

Mr. and Mrs. Brian G. Evans and Family

Marie Fay Evnochides

Frenchy and Jim Falik

Brian Falik

The Richard Finger Family

Clay, Carrie and Kelly Fisher

Grayson L. P. Fitch

The Floyd Family - Jeff, Robin,
Lindsay, Taylor and Lauren

The Ford Family - Ellen, Tommy and Elizabeth

Thomas W. and Cora Ford

Jill Fortney Productions, Inc.

The Fox Family - Sheryn, Bill, Amy and Lacey

Dr. and Mrs. Robert Frachtman and Family

The Frank Family - Mary John, Louise,
Catherine, Cathy and Ed

John and Karen Freeman and Family

Gilbert and Mary Kay Gaedcke

The Gage Family - Waverly, Bill,
Sara Jane, William and Hudson

Mrs. George P. Gardere, Jr. and Family

Mr. and Mrs. Robert Garey

The Garrison Family - Monroe,
Alicia, Thomas and Charles

Duke Gatlin

The Gaylor Family - Stuart, Anita,
Graham, Mollie and Sophie

Christine and Douglas Gehrman

The Gemp Family - Matthew, Alison,
Ian, Eric and Emily

Rev. and Mrs. John C. Gibbs

George and Nicole Nathan Gibson and Family

David Goddard and Ruth Goddard
in honor of Art Goddard

Jason Alan Goldstein

Edward Gorden

Cathey Speer Graham

Linda and John David Hagerman

Mr. and Mrs. Mark Hammer

Mr. and Mrs. John William Hancock III

The Harcrow Family

The Harris Family - Susan, Jon,
Rebecca and Sarah

Rosemary and Dan Harrison III

The Haverland Family - Bill, Nancy and Bill III

Mr. and Mrs. Dennis J. Hayden and Family

Ron and Sheri Henriksen

Sue and Bob Herman

The Herrings - Laura, Alyssa, Juliana,
Carroll and Lauren

Kirk Heyne and Karen Twitchell

The Family of Dave Hinds

Frank, Amy and Kate Hinnant

Merle and Peter Holland

Garrett A. Holloway

Paul T. Homsy, M.D., M.P.H.

Anne, Emily and Nellie Hoppe

Dorothy Knox Howe Houghton

The Hrncir Family - John, Betty,
Trent and Garrett

The James Family - Kendrick, Tany, Kendrick II,
Keller, Carson and Cameron

Elizabeth Jennings

Barbara Jogerst

Mr. and Mrs. Scott W. Johnson

John R. Johnston

Mr. and Mrs. Dennis Johnston and Family

The Kalmans Family - Elyse, Lewis,
Aerin, Kendall and Talia

The Kanellopoulos Family - Drew,
Bunny, Paul and Nicole

Mr. and Mrs. Huey C. Keeney

Chaille Cage Kelly

The Kelly Family - Mark, Kim, Kristin,
Ryan and Madeline

Bob and Sally Kent

Mr. and Mrs. F. Paul Khuri and Family

The Klevenhagen Family - JJ, Kim
and Courtney

Frances Koelsch

Robert Koelsch

Stephen Krivda

The Kuruvilla Family - Mohan, Sneha and Rohit

Mr. and Mrs. Henry J. Lartigue and Family

The Laswell Family - Gregg, Claudia,
Gregg, Nelson and Stephen

The Lattimer Family - Daniel, Julie,
Blake and Grayson

The Leavitt Family - Lewis,
Christopher and Lauren

The Lee Family - Brian, Michelle and Andrew

Jack and Susan Lee

Mr. and Mrs. Steven Leisz and Family

The Leonard Family - Michael,
Colette and David

The Leven Family - Debby, Harris,
Jeff and Jonathan

The Levy Family - Shauna, Carly, Andrew, Joanne and Bruce

Michael Lewitton and Allison Lipshultz

The Likover Family - Larry, Bonnie, Clay, Lee and Collin

Mr. and Mrs. Kyle D. Lippman

Lynn and Ellis Locher

The Lopez Family - David, Romelia and Vianei

David and Katherine Lucke

The Luening Family - Judann, Friedhelm and Christian

Joan E. H. Lyons

Mr. and Mrs. Robert Ted Lyons and Family

JoAnne Maby

The Mackay Family - Doug, Shelley, Blake and Julie

Dr. A.C. and Maria Marcaccio and Graham Gaylor

Joanne and Ross Margraves

Clyde and Ann Marsau

The Marsh Family - Bill, Julie, Lauren and Lindsay

The Mason Family - Gavin, Andrea, Owen, Glen and Anna Ciara

Brian Massingill

Mr. and Mrs. Drew Masterson and Family

Garry Mc Millan

Megan Metcalf

Stephen Miles, Jr.

The Miller Family - Michael, Ingrid and Jenny

The Mings Family - John, Kara, Mason and Kaylie

Palmer and Susanna Moldawer, Matthew, Ben and Eliza

Jane Hoffert Moore

The Moore Family - Tom, Jennifer and Eddie

Christine and Shea Morenz

Walter A. Muller

Dorian St. Clair Myers

Dr. and Mrs. Cesar and Liliane Nahas

Elizabeth Topper Nash

The Nishikawa Family - Akira, Minami, Mia and Millie

Katherine Hankamer Norris

Betty Nan and Herman (Obe) Obermayer

The Odom Family - Trey, Stacey, Blake and Adair

Mr. and Mrs. Robert Orkin and Family

Mr. and Mrs. David P. Orr and Family

Martha and Jose Oti

R.L. Pardue Family - Diana, Frank, Lee and Missy

Dr. and Mrs. Bradford S. Patt

The Patton Family - Barbara, John, John W. and Polly

Elwin M. Peacock

Philip and Julie Peacock

Mary Bain Haralson Pearson

Mr. and Mrs. Michael P. Pearson

The Peppas Family - Nicholas, Lisa, Katia and Alexi

The Perkins Family - Delman, Jean and Robert

The Pullen Family - Bob, Anne, Robert, Wesley, Elizabeth Schwing and Corey

The Racusin Family - Charles, Estelle and Ben

John A. Rathmell

Mr. and Mrs John B. Reckling and Family

The Ribbeck Family - Craig, Rachel, Catherine and Molly

The Richardson Family - Suzann, Terry, Blair, and Will

Mr. and Mrs. Corbin J. Robertson, Jr. and Family - Corby III, Christine and Will

Tavenner and Sean Rogers

The Rome Family - Mike, Merrill, Hunter, Hayden and Harris

The Roseman Family - Barbara, Donald and Gavin

The Rubinsky Family - Lisa, Abrey, Adam and Alana

The Rude Family - David, Roberta, Hayner and Lloyd

The Sandvig Family - Doug, Mary, Kristen and David

The Schroeder Family - Walt, Maggie, Claire and Brian

The Schuenemann Family - Kim, Kyle, Thomas and Blaise

The Schuette Family - Dawn, John, Allison and Jack

Richard and Criss Scruggs

Daniel and Lisa Falik Seigle

The Selzer Family - Karen, Bill, Morgan and Cory

The Zack Semander Family

Sue and Steve Shaper

The Sheedy Family - Charles, Ellen, Elizabeth, Patrick, Colleen, Laura and Andrew

The Sheehy Family - Richard, Madeleine, Topper, Patrick and Reilly

The Singh Family - Indar, Indra and Perveen

Kimberly Skipton

Clark and Barbara Smith

Mr. and Mrs. Stacy A. Smith

Lucas B. Somoza

The Sowell Family - Andy, Sherra, Rachel and Jackson

William B. Stanberry, Jr.

Mr. and Mrs. Franklin T. Stevenson

Annie Ray Watkin Strange

Mr. and Mrs. Jack Stubbs and Family

Mersina Pappas Stubbs

Mr. and Mrs. Jason N. Sweeney

Dr. and Mrs. James Tang

The Taylor Family - Larry, Laura, Dean and Barrett

Lorenzo B. Taylor

The Taylor Family - Terry, Lori, Tessa, Mikaela and Tyson

Ford and Lauri Thanheiser

The Thompson Family - Scott, Candy, Traci and Scotty

The Tillison Family - Craig, Jennifer and Stephanie

The Tiner Family - Michael, Betti, Kristen and Keri

Robert and Stephanie Tobor

Doug and Diane Trahan

The Tucker Family - Bob, Hilary, Ali and Austin

The Lee Tuttle Family

The van Keppel Family

Ellen and Robert Wagnon

John and Yvonne Wallace

The Wallace Family - Tim, Sally, Caroline and Sara Jane

The Tucker Family - Bob, Hilary, Ali and Austin

The Warmington Family

Leslye, David, Alexander and Suzanne Weaver

Dede and Connie Weil

Dr. and Mrs. Stuart Weil

Ellen Welsh - Hope and Charlotte Morales

Mr. and Mrs. Milton H. West III

Mr. and Mrs. R. Graham Whaling

Mr. and Mrs. Robert Whilden and Family

Ben and Lindsey Whitman

Marilyn Wilhelm

The Williams Family - Blake, Christine, Georgia, Bain and Mary Blake

Cynthia Joanne Wilson

Joanne and Welcome Wilson

Ellen E. Wilson

Steven and Sandi Wolf

Russell P. Wynings, Jr. - In Memory of Donna F. Wynings

The Younger Family

Nicole and David Zarr

The Zody Family - Chuck, Diana and Mike

* As of August 26, 2005

Steve Adger ('67)
Diana Armbrust
Brad Armstrong ('77)
Doug Aron ('92)
Roni Atnipp
John B. Baird III ('57)
Lucy Hutcheson Barrow ('77)
Patricia Hamilton Bivins ('85)
Robert L. Bradley, Jr. ('73)
Katie Mattingly Brass ('90)
Kasey Buza ('98)
Nadia Campbell ('03)
Lucy Carl
A.J. Carothers ('50)
Kathleen Carson ('67)
Heather Fichter Cassidy ('78)
Dunbar N. Chambers III ('77)
Bonnie German Chandler ('69)
Erminie Chambers Chapman ('49)
Catherine Choate Christopherson ('75)
Ashley Brunson Clark ('87)
Drew and Beth Cozby
Robert Cronin ('60)
Emily Attwell Crosswell ('59)
Linda Beeley Denison ('58)
Nancy Dinerstein
Katherine Shanks Dodd
Lisa Castle Donnell ('75)
Barbara Drell
Holt Dunlop ('92)
Allison Allbritton Dwyer ('90)
Louise Pincoffs Ellingson ('39)
Emory D. Ellsworth ('81)
Clark Kent Ervin ('77)
Marie Fay Evnochides ('59)
Canaan Factor ('96)
Jonathan Finger ('78)
Carrie Harp Fisher
Rebecca Brunson Flannery ('91)
Robert E. Fondren ('80)
Elizabeth Ford ('12)
Lynn Meyer Fort ('68)
Waverly White Gage ('82)

Anita M. Gaylor
Connie Giles
Paul, Dana, Ryan ('08) and Travis Gill
Betsy LaFuze Gill ('96)
Tom Glass
Dorothy Turner Glauser ('35)
Dr. Joanna Gol ('77)
John J. Gorden ('74)
Nancy Gordon
Makeea Frazier Grainger
John David Hagerman ('59)
Stephanie Luther Hamilton
Frank and Amy Hinnant
Winifred Wheeler Hinnant ('53)
Dorthy Knox Howe Houghton ('62)
Katherine Susman Howe ('64)
Kate Howe ('95)
Carrie Iglehart ('91)
Dr. Stuart Jacobson ('78)
Hector Janse ('50)
J. Webb Jennings III ('89)
Frances Hopper Jeter ('74)
Sally Dudley Kent ('70)
Martha Lartigue
Marline Lawson
Dr. Betty Lee
Louis and Beverly Lerner
Judy Levin ('75)
Allison Maricelli Loukanis ('78)
Mary Nell Jeffers Lovett ('63)
Jane Wadsworth Mason ('63)
Patricia McCall ('50)
Christiana Reckling McConn
Lila Luckie McCall ('51)
Ginny Merrifield
Rain Minns ('93)
Tom Moore
Bethany Morehouse ('00)
Christine Robertson Morenz ('92)
Dinnie Smith Mowery ('36)
Judy Muir
J.R. Neiswender ('89)
Joanna Semander Nicolaou ('84)

Eleni Pappas ('04)
Virginia Lawhon Park ('55)
Mary Bain Haralson Pearson ('49)
Kate Petley ('72)
Cindi Wilson Proler ('71)
Peter Raspler ('87)
Corby and Barbara Moses Robertson ('65)
Vianei Lopez Robinson ('85)
Charles L. Roff ('79)
Drs. Mary Katharine and John H. Roff III ('76)
Janie Rommel-Eichorn ('63)
Michael Rose ('64)
Howard Rosenberg
Robert Rowley ('75)
Charles B. Sanders, Jr. ('54)
Kathy Sangalis
Susan Hillebrandt Santangelo ('55)
Elyse Schultz
Kathy McAnelly Schwartz ('79)
Kate Lovett Searls ('93)
Phyllis Selber
John Semander ('88)
Josephine Muller Shanks ('51)
Laura Leigh Smith
Mark Sorrell ('74)
Stephen Spivey ('90)
Leslie Sprague
Sarijane "Sassy" English Stanton ('60)
Melissa Miller Stonebrook ('77)
Annie Ray Watkin Strange ('30)
Ellen Rothermel Stuart ('59)
Dr. James Tang ('66)
Anne Thomson
Dr. Joseph H. Thywissen ('91)
Bronwyn Burke Tilton ('89)
Dr. Lee L.D. Tuttle, Jr. ('49)
J.C. "Rusty" Walter III ('76)
Leslye Lucas Weaver
F.T. (Chip) Webster ('66)
Courtney Wilson ('99)
Welcome Wilson, Jr. ('69)
Cindy Witmer
Betsy Wittenmyer

Josephine Abercrombie ('42)
Audrey Reynolds Alexander ('62)
Lee Allbritton ('85)
John Anderson ('64)
Ginger Armbrust ('76)
Daniel C. Arnold ('47)
Jennifer Tuttle Arnold ('78)
James A. Baker III ('48)
Dr. Robert T. Baldwin ('77)
Thomas Barrow ('41)
Adam Battelstein ('81)
Audrey Jones Beck ('39)
George Bellows ('42)
Tom Bellows ('73)
Pat Paukune Berry ('80)
Ray Biggers ('90)
Patricia Hamilton Bivins ('85)
Laura Lee Scurlock Blanton ('46)
Dr. William A. Blattner ('62)
Melissa Wadler Bloome ('92)
Robert Bradley, Jr. ('73)
Lisa Brannon-Peppas ('80)
Zachry Brown ('02)
President George W. Bush ('64)
Governor Jeb Bush ('70)
Nadia Campbell ('03)
William Noble Carl, Jr. ('55)
William Noble Carl III ('83)
A.J. Carothers ('50)
Gibson Carothers ('62)
Lindsay Carr ('00)
Charles Carson ('65)
Kathleen Carson ('67)
John Cassidy ('68)
Dunbar Chambers III ('77)
Catherine Choate Christopherson ('75)
Ann Tharp Clifford ('54)
Warren Coles ('76)
Mary Frances Bowles Couper ('28)
Maria Semander Crawford ('82)
Peter Creath ('93)
Robert Cronin ('60)
David Crossley ('57)
Emily Attwell Crosswell ('59)
O. Holcombe Crosswell ('58)
Ellen Lloyd Cummins ('77)
Charlotte Williams Darby ('21)
Adelaide DeMenil ('53)
Phyllis Childs Detering ('33)
William Detering, Jr. ('75)
Julia Gregg DeWalch ('81)
Charles Dillingham ('62)
Ross Dinerstein ('97)
Betty Dudley
Thomas Dunlap ('80)
Louise Pincoffs Ellingson ('39)
Adam Ereli ('79)
Clark Kent Ervin ('77)
Mary Elizabeth Winfrey Evans ('96)
Marie Fay Evnochides ('59)
Jackie Fair ('84)
Carolyn Grant Fay ('29)
Dr. David Finegold ('81)
Jonathan Finger ('78)
Walter W. Fondren III ('54)
Tom Ford ('42)
Billy Forney ('92)
Pam Wilson Francis ('73)
Peter Gardere ('88)
Jonathan Gaw ('02)
Cullen Geiselman ('93)
Jackie Gendel ('92)
Keith Gendel ('90)
David Gerger ('78)
Mike German ('75)
Dorothy Turner Glauser ('35)
Dr. Joanna Gol ('77)
Chip Goodyear ('76)

Ryan Gordon ('93)
Diane Asbury Gordon ('59)
George Grainger ('76)
Amy Grant ('78)
Brad Harman ('87)
Pamela Hay ('95)
Lynn McLanhan Hebert ('74)
Dan Hedges ('64)
Robine Smulders Hendricks ('90)
Scott Heumann ('69)
Winifred Bain Wheeler Hinnant ('53)
William P. Hobby, Jr. ('49)
Edwin Hornberger ('39)
David Hornsby ('94)
Dorothy Knox Howe Houghton ('62)
Katherine Susman Howe ('64)
Thad Hutcheson ('30)
Tany Hopper James ('80)
Dick Janse ('54)
Francis Hopper Jeter ('74)
Burdine Clayton Johnson ('26)
Yoav Kaufman ('98)
Thomas E. Kelly ('49)
Mimi Smith Kilgore ('53)
Frannie Koelsch ('85)
Caroline Wiess Law ('35)
Virginia Vinson Lawhon ('27)
Rusty Lerner ('83)
Chris Little ('59)
Susie Loucks ('77)
Mary Nell Jeffers Lovett ('63)
Gerre Gillespie Lucas ('39)
Alan Luther ('88)
Allison Marich ('77)
Jeff Martin ('78)
Jane Wadsworth Mason ('63)
Carroll Sterling Masterson ('28)
Harris Masterson ('28)
Lila Luckie McCall ('51)
Patricia McCall ('50)
Carolyn McCormick ('77)
Robin Hunt McCorquodale ('52)
Mike McDougal ('64)
Dr. Margaret McNeese ('63)
Kelly Sweeney McShane ('83)
Marshall Merrifield ('78)
Alice Baker Jones Meyer ('31)
Joseph F. Meyer III ('36)
Susu Zimmerman Meyer ('73)
Rain Minns ('93)
Michael Minns ('69)
Susan Monk ('85)
Jeffrey Morehouse ('98)
Rob Moreland ('83)
Dinnie Smith Mowery ('36)
Chad Muir ('88)
Shawn Nacol ('88)
Ashleigh Nankivell ('99)
Susan Neptune ('66)
Betty Bosworth Neuhaus ('38)
Angie North ('98)
Clint O'Connor ('74)
Brian Ogilvie ('00)
Gail Wolf Orr ('81)
Dr. Melissa O'Toole ('82)
Carter Overton ('80)
Annie Owen ('68)
Jane Blaffer Owen ('30)
Mary Pappas ('93)
Evy Pappas ('94)
Robbin Parish ('61)
Elwin Peacock ('44)
Susan Storey Peake ('79)
Mary Bain Haralson Pearson ('49)
Kate Petley ('72)
Virginia Pittman-Waller ('80)
Scott Prescott ('73)
Peter Raspler ('87)

Adam Raspler ('89)
Sep Riahi ('85)
Browne and Ann Townes Rice ('39)
Beth Robertson ('64)
Vianei Lopez Robinson ('85)
Jennifer Deal Rogers ('89)
Mary Jane Hale Rommel ('31)
Charles B. Sanders, Jr. ('54)
Dr. Sherri Sandifer ('91)
Susan Hillebrandt Santangelo ('55)
Peter Schlumberger ('59)
Dr. George Schudy ('62)
Eryn Schultz ('04)
Chuck Scofield ('88)
Vernon Scott ('79)
Scott Sears ('62)
Harriett Semander
Glenn Seureau ('59)
Josephine Muller Shanks ('51)
C. Park Shaper ('86)
Marc J. Shapiro ('65)
Scott Shapiro ('87)
Brett Simchowitz ('01)
Ashley Smith ('64)
Chris Smith ('99)
Frank C. Smith, Jr. ('38)
Wilhelmina Cullen Robertson Smith ('40)
Mauvirine Sorrell
Dr. Cedric Spak ('90)
Spence Spencer ('80)
Sarijane "Sassy" English Stanton ('60)
Annette Faubion Stephens ('82)
Philip Stephenson ('83)
Annie Ray Watkin Strange ('30)
John Suman ('35)
Johnny Sutton ('79)
Dr. James Tang ('66)
Laurye Rutten Tanner ('67)
Marianne Tatum ('69)
Patrick Gayman Taylor ('55)
Giggy Martin Thanheiser ('77)
Dr. Joseph H. Thywissen ('91)
Lisa Tuttle ('70)
Francita Stuart Koelsch Ulmer ('49)
David M. Underwood ('54)
Brian Van DeMark ('78)
Dr. William Van Vorst ('36)
Caro Ivy Walker ('46)
Walter T. Weathers III ('89)
Alison Webster ('94)
Steve Weingarten ('75)
Damon Wells ('54)
Jill Wiley White ('89)
Alex Whittington ('99)
Emily Tuttle Wilde ('80)
Marilyn Wilhelm ('50)
Temple Williams ('83)
Welcome Wilson, Jr. ('69)
Travis Winfrey ('95)
Eula Goss Winterman ('27)
Bettina Yang ('88)
Dr. Russell Yang ('74)
Neil Zimmerman ('95)

# PHOTOGRAPHY CAPTIONS

**FRONT FLY SHEET**
Erik Eisele ('00)

**PAGE 3**
Kinkaid graduates,
1950's

**PAGE 5**
Kindergarten and Low First students at
Mrs. Kinkaid's home, 1912: top L-R:
unknown, James Bowles, Malcolm
Cravens, George Baker, unknown, Zaidee
Lee Foster, Dorothy Boettcher, unknown,
Virginia Gibbs, Mrs. Kinkaid; (remaining
students unknown)

**PAGE 16**
Students lunching under
the trees, 1940

**PAGE 19**
1940's students on the Richmond
Avenue campus: L-R: Harriet Carlton,
Emmy Coates, Marcia Lambert, Sarah
Faulkner, Chaille Walsh, Barbara Smith,
Susan Janse, Virginia Jago, Bonner
Baker, Jerry Lollar

**PAGES 20-21**
Balloon Day, 1980's

**PAGES 22-23**
Graduating class of 1932: top L-R: Albert Sterling,
William Cochran, Jr., Lucille Meachum, Mary
Margaret Dudley, Betty Brann, Ruth Granberry,
Mary Greenwood; middle L-R: unknown, Katherine
Pillot, Polly Pruter, Margaret Turner; front L-R:
Rosemary Watkin, Nancy Smith, Amelia Duncan,
Frederick Rorsodi

**PAGE 32**
top: Ann Goar Campbell ('53) and George Birks ('55) in *Pirates
of Penzance,* 1953; bottom: cast of *Pirates of Penzance,* 1953

**PAGE 33**
Tom Boyd staging a drama production, 1966: L-R: Marshall
Echols, Carter Hood, Bill Fogle, Anne Lents, Stan Erck,
Margaret Frederking, Tom Boyd, Diane Martin

**PAGE 54**
William Kinkaid, 1940's

**PAGES 58-59**
Student performance at Miller Outdoor Theatre,
1920's

**PAGE 71**
Kinkaid cheerleading
pep rally, 1983

**PAGE 72**
Large oak tree on the
Richmond Avenue
campus, 1930

**PAGE 80**
top left: long jumper, 1941; top right: archery class, 1950; middle left: football player, 1941; middle right:
boxing lessons, 1939 (a young James A. Baker III and William P. Hobby, Jr., with teacher Jack Arnold); bottom
left: girls' softball, 1930; bottom right: 1947 cheerleaders Sally Logue, Joan Herrin and Jane Gwathemy

**PAGE 81**
top left: 1941 six-man football team (top L-R: Bob Tenison, David Pollan, Gene Hovey, George Bellows;
bottom L-R: Hendley Tomlinson, Harvey Houck, Joe Brown); top right: 1978 Middle School cheerleaders
Elizabeth Pullen, Darby Denison and Cindy Coates; middle left: 1957 Elementary basketball champions
Jack Isbell ('63) and Randy Meyer ('63); middle right: baseball, 1950; bottom left: girls' volleyball, 1950;
bottom right: George Bellows ('42) as a member of the 1941 six-man football team

**PAGES 82-83**
2004 senior boys showing their Falcon spirit at
the October 2003 Kinkaid-St. John's football game:
L-R: John Bell, Brian Kaplan, Charles Barbour,
Walt Lundell, Jeff Feinstein, Bailey Pouns, Price
Harmon, Daniel Romero, Matthew Kaufman

**PAGE 90**

The Cookie and Candy Booth at Field Day, 2000: L-R: Betty Dudley, Burt Meyer

**PAGE 97**

Second grade students, 1983: bottom to top: Rob Vermillion, Emily Witt, Lara Muir, Will Fogle, Marshall Harrison, Christy Iglehart, Stephanie Friedman, James Whitehead, Cathy Angerstein, Kim Sweeney, Lizzie Carrell, Ford O'Connell, Scott Gordon

**PAGE 98**

Fifth grade students, 1919-1920: back L-R: Joe Short, unknown, Alvus Armstrong, Malcolm Cravens; middle L-R: Ella Campbell Horton, Dorothy Scott, Maxine Schnitzer, Maud Gray Hester; front L-R: Annie Mae, Rachel Naples, Ruth Naples

**PAGE 99**

Fifth grade students, 2005: back L-R: Max Scheinin, Macan Wilson, William Berry, Ryan Clegg; middle L-R: Brianna Allen, Mabry Bolin, Priya Afzalpurkar, Sophia Overton; bottom L-R: Kristen Cummins, Victoria Wang, Lola Martins

**PAGES 100-101**

Elizabeth Paton, teacher of Latin, on the Richmond Avenue campus, 1950's

**PAGE 112**

Middle School students singing in study hall, Richmond Avenue campus, 1949

**PAGE 113**

Lower School library, Richmond Avenue campus, 1940's

**PAGE 125**

1942 graduating class

**PAGES 132-133**

1921 faculty at the school on Elgin Street: top L-R: Mrs. Ballinger, writing teacher, Mrs. Albrecht, Mrs. Lee, Low First teacher, Mrs. Kinkaid; front L-R: Mrs. Kelsey, Miss Cook, Miss Rosenblatt

**PAGE 134**

top left: Celina Kilpatrick, 1980's; top right: Patty Edwards, 2005; middle left: Jerome Doswell; middle right: Ruth Ereli and Middle School students, 2005; bottom left: Gene Festa, 2005; bottom right: Gerald Perkins in biology class, 1980's

**PAGE 135**

top left: Emma Jane Miller, 1970's; top right: Kathryn Wade with math students, 2005; middle left: Bonnie Hetrick in Health Center, 2005; middle right: Alicia Woodhams, 1980's; bottom left: J. Barry Moss, 1980's; bottom right: Greg Gephart

**PAGES 140-141**

Coach Jack Hanagriff and 1952 sixth grade City Championship football team

**PAGE 143**

Don North and prekindergarten kids at Halloween, 2002

**PAGE 160**

Mrs. Kinkaid, 1940's

**BACK FLY SHEET**

Kinkaid bell created by Pat Foley

# PHOTOGRAPHY CREDITS

## THE HISTORY

Front fly sheet: Erik Eisele ('00), from 1989-1990 Annual Report*

Pg 3: Kinkaid graduates, 1950's*

Pg 5: Kindergarten and Low First students at Mrs. Kinkaid's home, 1912*

Pg 6: Portrait of Mrs. Kinkaid painted by Robert Joy, commissioned by the Class of 1946, photographed by Fred Keinz

Pg 8: top: Margaret Kinkaid, age 18*; Inset: Margaret Kinkaid and son William, 1916*

Pg 9: Margaret Kinkaid and her husband, William, on vacation, 1920*

Pg 11: Portrait of John Cooper painted by James Wills in 1978*

Pg 12: Glenn Ballard and Dolly visiting with Lower School students, 1984*

Pg 13: Glenn Ballard at 1985 Commencement, by Rob Muir, from 1996 spring issue of the *Kinkaid Magazine*

Pg 14: Don North in the Brown Auditorium, by Fred Keinz, from 2002 Special Edition of the *Kinkaid Magazine*

Pg 15: Don North visiting with Lower School students in his office, 1999*

Pg 16: Students lunching under the trees, 1940*

Pg 19: 1940's students on the Richmond Avenue campus*

Pgs 20-21: Balloon Day, 1980's*

## THE ALUMNI

Pgs 22-23: Graduating class of 1932*

Pg 24: Josephine Abercrombie ('42), by Bourdon, 1940*

Pg 25: Daniel C. Arnold ('47), by Melissa DeAyala, from 1998 spring issue of the *Kinkaid Magazine*

Pg 26: James A. Baker III ('48) speaking at 1985 Commencement, by Rob Muir*

Pg 27: Thomas D. Barrow ('41), provided by Tom Barrow

Pg 28: Audrey Jones Beck ('39), provided by Museum of Fine Arts, Houston

Pg 29: George Bellows ('42), by Gittings, 1942*

Pg 30: Laura Lee Scurlock Blanton ('46), from 1946 Kinkaid yearbook

Pg 31: Dr. William Blattner ('62) at the opening of the ARV treatment center at the Nnamdi Azikiwe Teaching Hospital, provided by Bill Blattner

Pg 32: top: Students in *Pirates of Penzance,* 1953*; bottom: Cast of *Pirates of Penzance,* 1953*

Pg 33: Tom Boyd staging a drama production, 1966*

Pg 34: Lisa Brannon-Peppas ('80), by Melissa DeAyala, from 1998 spring issue of the *Kinkaid Magazine*

Pg 37: President George W. Bush ('64) on the 1960 freshman football team, from 1961 Kinkaid yearbook

Pg 38: Governor Jeb Bush ('70), provided by Jeb Bush

Pg 39: A. J. Carothers ('50), by Walt Disney Productions, 1963*

Pg 40: Gibson Carothers ('62), provided by Gibson Carothers

Pg 41: Charles Carson ('65) working in Africa as a volunteer for Living Water International, provided by Charles Carson

Pg 42: John Cassidy ('68), provided by John Cassidy

Pg 43: Mary Frances Bowles Couper ('28), 1964, provided by Mary Frances Couper

Pg 44: Robert Cronin ('60) in his workshop, 1987, provided by Robert Cronin

Pg 45: Holcombe Crosswell ('58) and Emily Attwell Crosswell ('59), provided by the Crosswells

Pg 46: Charles Dillingham ('61), provided by Charles Dillingham

Pg 47: Adam Ereli ('79) at US State Department briefings, provided by Adam Ereli

Pg 48: Clark Kent Ervin ('77), provided by Clark Ervin

Pg 49: Marie Fay Evnochides ('59), provided by Marie Evnochides

Pg 50: David Louis Finegold ('81), provided by David Finegold

Pg 51: Walter W. Fondren III ('54), provided by Walter Fondren

Pg 52: Cullen Geiselman ('93), Wilhelmina Cullen Smith ('40) and Beth Robertson ('64), by Susan Davis Johnson ('65), from 1993 spring issue of the *Kinkaid Magazine*

Pg 54: William Kinkaid, 1940's*

Pg 55: Scott Heumann ('69), by John Everett, from September 27, 1992, issue of the *Houston Chronicle*

Pg 56: William P. Hobby, Jr. ('49), provided by Bill Hobby

Pg 57: Katherine Susman Howe ('64), provided by Katherine Howe

Pgs 58-59: Student performance at Miller Outdoor Theatre, 1920's*

Pg 60: Thaddeus Thomson Hutcheson ('30), by Gittings, provided by his daughter, Lucy Hutcheson Barrow ('77)

Pg 61: Thomas E. Kelly ('49), by Ward W. Wells for the *Anchorage Times* announcing Tom's 1967 appointment as Commissioner of Natural Resources of Alaska, provided by Tom Kelly

Pg 62: Emilie "Mimi" Smith Kilgore ('53) at her Houston Country Club debut party, late 1950's, provided by Mimi Kilgore

Pg 63: Caroline Wiess Law ('35) at the ribbon-cutting ceremony for MFAH's new administration building, 1994, provided by Museum of Fine Arts, Houston

Pg 64: Christopher M. Little ('59), provided by Chris Little

Pg 65: Mary Nell Jeffers Lovett ('63), by Temple Webber, 1996

Pg 66: Allison Marich ('77) performing onstage in *The Seagull,* 1988, by Buddy Myers, provided by Allison Marich

Pg 67: Jeff Martin ('78) in his David Letterman office, 1983, provided by Jeff Martin

Pg 68: Carroll Sterling Masterson ('28) and Harris Masterson ('28), provided by the Museum of Fine Arts, Houston

Pg 69: Carolyn McCormick ('77), provided by Carolyn McCormick

Pg 70: Margaret C. McNeese ('63), provided by Margaret McNeese

Pg 71: Kinkaid cheerleading pep rally, 1983*

Pg 72: Large oak tree on the Richmond Avenue campus, 1930*

Pg 73: Kelly Sweeney McShane ('83), from 1983 Kinkaid yearbook

Pg 74: Marshall Merrifield ('78), provided by Marshall Merrifield and Playground Partners

Pg 75: Dinnie Smith Mowery ('36), 1952, provided by Dinnie Mowery

Pg 76: Anne Dale Owen ('68), Abigail Owen-Pontez ('08) and Jane Blaffer Owen ('30), taken by Melissa DeAyala at the 2000 Distinguished Alumni Dinner*

Pg 77: Robbin Parish ('61), provided by Robbin Parish

Pg 78: Vianei Lopez Robinson ('85), by Kugler Studios, provided by Vianei Robinson

Pg 79: Chuck Scofield ('88) in Ethiopia, provided by Chuck Scofield

Pg 80: top left: long jumper, 1941*; top right: archery class, 1950, by Stiles*; middle left: football player, 1941*; middle right: boxing lessons, 1939*; bottom left: girls' softball, 1930*; bottom right: 1947 cheerleaders*

Pg 81: top left: 1941 six-man football team*; 1978 Middle School cheerleaders, by Francis Shepherd*; middle left: 1957 Elementary basketball champions*; middle right: baseball, 1950*; bottom left: girls' volleyball, 1950*; bottom right: George Bellows ('42) as a member of the 1941 six-man football team*

Pgs 82-83: 2004 senior boys showing their Falcon spirit at the October 2003 Kinkaid-St. John's football game*

Pg 84: Vernon Scott ('79), by Fred Keinz, featured on the cover of the 1994 winter issue of the *Kinkaid Magazine*

Pg 85: Admiral Scott Sears ('62), provided by Scott Sears

Pg 86: Marc J. Shapiro ('65), provided by Marc Shapiro

Pg 87: Johnny Sutton ('79) as a 1981 University of Texas Longhorn baseball player, by Jon Fory, provided by Johnny Sutton

Pg 88: Marianne Tatum ('69) as Jenny Lind in the Broadway musical *Barnum,* by Martha Swope, provided by Marianne Tatum

Pg 90: Betty Dudley and Burt Meyer in the Cookie and Candy Booth at Field Day, 2000*

Pg 91: Patrick F. Taylor ('55), provided by Patrick Taylor's office, from 2004 summer issue of the *Kinkaid Magazine*

Pg 92: Joseph H. Thywissen ('91), provided by Joseph Thywissen

Pg 93: David M. Underwood ('54), 1992, by Kaye Marvins, provided by David Underwood

Pg 94: William D. Van Vorst ('36), provided by William Van Vorst

Pg 95: Damon Wells ('54) delivering the valedictorian address at commencement on May 21, 1954, provided by Damon Wells

Pg 96: Temple Williams ('83), by Fred Keinz, from 2003 spring issue of the *Kinkaid Magazine*

Pg 97: Second grade students, 1983*

## THE TIMELINE

Pgs 98: Fifth grade students, 1919-1920*

Pg 99: Fifth grade students, 2005, by Fred Keinz

Timeline panel one: Mrs. Kinkaid's home / school on Elgin and San Jacinto Streets, drawing by Dennis Shepler; Sixth grade graduating class of 1917*; the first school newspaper – *The Kinkaid Almanac*; Jennifer Smith ('60), from 1960 Kinkaid yearbook*; AFS students Gunilla Hedman and Georg Riedinger, from 1962 Kinkaid yearbook*; 1961 Freshman Class Officers David Hedges, Mike Rose and George Bush, from 1961 Kinkaid yearbook*; Commencement on the athletic field, 1993*; Class of 1974 Phonathon callers Pat Frede, Steve Turtur, Madeleine Topper Sheehy and Jed Goodall, 1983*; Don North with Leon Weiner, Reverend William Lawson, Sandra Weiner and Rachel Weiner Davis ('75), 2000 spring issue of the *Kinkaid Magazine*;

Timeline panel two: Richmond Avenue campus, 1940's*; William Kinkaid, 1940's*; The "Little Gym," by Charles B. Sanders, Jr.*; Mike Robinson ('70) munching on a survival cracker, 1969*; Dee Berryman and students, 1980*; Moran Library,

1971*; Middle School dedication program, 1992*; Scott Lambert and Patty Edwards with the 1994 Texas Forensic Association Championship trophy, 1994, by Fred Keinz*; lacrosse players, 1994*; Steve Retzloff ('74) and Zack Semander at the first alumni golf tournament, 1998, by Lynn Fort

Timeline panel three: Henry Anderson, Bill Brown, Maconda Brown and Mike Kelley selling war bonds, 1944*; All-male graduating class of 1948: L-R: Jim Greene, Tom Eaton, Jack McAninch, Bob Hill, Edwin Allday, Bob Gossett, Joe Baldwin*; Picture postcard of the Memorial campus, 1957*; Dr. Damon Wells and Wells Fellow James Michener, 1984*; Pat Foley sculpture that stood in front of the Holcombe Lower School Library*; construction picture of San Felipe extension over the Buffalo Bayou, 1974, by Bill Murchison*; Members of the 1973-74 Spirit of Kinkaid club (SOK), from 1974 Kinkaid yearbook; 1998 Rice scoreboard for the Kinkaid-St. John's football game from the cover of the 1999 winter issue of the *Kinkaid Magazine*; Japanese geisha performing for the first Lower School International Fair, 2000 spring issue of the

*Kinkaid Magazine*; 2001 swim team champions, from 2001 Kinkaid yearbook; Character Education Director Mike Pardee in the entrance foyer to the Center for Student Life, Fine Arts and Administration Building, 2004, by Fred Keinz

Timeline panel four: First elected Mr. and Miss Falcon: Virginia Joy and John Elias, from 1958 Kinkaid yearbook; cast members from Kinkaid's first Shakespearean play, *Hamlet*, from 1958 Kinkaid yearbook; Kinkaid students, 1950*; Jane Owen, Camilla Blaffer ('59), Rev. Charles Wyatt Brown, Jane Blaffer Owen ('30) and John Cooper at the groundbreaking ceremony for the new Performing Arts Building, 1975*; the Tintoretto painting, *The Baptism of Christ*; Balcony view of the Brown Auditorium, 2003, by Fred Keinz; Donnie Morgan Clock Tower and the Center for Student Life, Fine Arts and Administration building, 2004, by Fred Keinz; the Kinkaid band members in China, 2004, provided by Fred Angerstein; drama students performing *Trojan Women* on the stage in Scotland, 2004, provided by Scott Lambert

## THE FACULTY AND STAFF

Pgs 100-101: Elizabeth Paton, teacher of Latin, on the Richmond Avenue campus, 1950's*

Pg 102: Fred Angerstein teaching band, 1980's, by Leiber Photography*

Pg 103: G'Ann and Tom Boyd, from 1966 Kinkaid yearbook

Pg 104: Coach Jan Braden with members of the 2002 field hockey team, from 2002 winter issue of the *Kinkaid Magazine*

Pg 105: Ann Tharp Clifford, from 1959 Kinkaid yearbook

Pg 106: Barbara Cooney with Middle School students in the library, 1980's, by Leiber Photography*

Pg 109: Joyce Crowl with second grade students, 1984*

Pg 110: Pat Foley with art student Mary Lou Kaufhold, 1974*

Pg 111: John and Caro Ann Germann, 2005, by Fred Keinz

Pg 112: Middle School students singing in study hall, Richmond Avenue campus, 1949*

Pg 113: Lower School library, Richmond Avenue campus, 1940's*

Pg 114: Art Goddard with Middle School students Mike Monk, Negin Riahi and Courtney Robbins in the hallway, 1983*

Pg 115: Esther Holt, 2005, by Fred Keinz

Pg 116: Ava Hooks, from 1959 Kinkaid yearbook

Pg 117: Mary Jones with kindergarten students, provided by Mary Jones

Pg 118: Katherine Leathem in The Kinkaid Backyard, 2005, by Fred Keinz

Pg 119: Eddie and Georgia Leonard, 1990's, provided by Georgia Leonard

Pg 120: Garry McMillan in the Moran Library with 1986 football captains Bryce Phillips, Richard Williams and Park Shaper*

Pg 121: J. Barry Moss, 1980's*

Pg 122: Fred Northcutt and Linda Miller in their classrooms, 2005, by Fred Keinz

Pg 123: Tom Peden in his Middle School classroom, 2005, by Lynn Fort

Pg 124: Rusty Ross ('91) with Charlie Sanders in the Kinkaid archives room

Pg 125: 1942 graduating class*

Pg 127: Susan Santangelo, 2005, by Lynn Fort

Pg 128: Phyllis Selber, 2005, by Fred Keinz

Pg 129: Harriet and Zack Semander at Zack's retirement party, 1995*

Pg 130: Louise Shreckengaust, from 1962 Kinkaid yearbook

Pg 131: Mary Vaughan, from 1972 Kinkaid yearbook

Pgs 132-133: 1921 faculty at the School on Elgin Street*

Pg 134: top left: Celina Kilpatrick, 1980's*; top right: Patty Edwards, 2005, by Lynn Fort; middle left: Jerome Doswell*; middle right: Ruth Ereli and Middle School students, 2005, by Lynn Fort; Botton left: Gene Festa, 2005, by Lynn Fort; bottom right: Gerald Perkins in biology class, 1980's*

Pg 135: top left: Emma Jane Miller, 1970's*; top right: Kathryn Wade with math students, 2005, by Lynn Fort; middle left: Bonnie Hetrick in HealthCenter, 2005, by Lynn Fort; middle right: Alicia Woodhams, 1980's*; bottom left: J. Barry Moss, 1980's*; bottom right: Greg Gephart, provided by Mary North

Pg 136: David and Deborah Veselka in The Kinkaid Backyard, 2005, by Fred Keinz

Pg 137: Leigh Weld, 1980's, by Leiber Photography *

Pg 138: Tom Wey, provided by Tom Wey

Pg 139: Sam Windsor teaching a Middle School math class, 1980's, by Leiber Photography*

Pgs 140-141: Coach Jack Hanagriff and 1952 sixth grade City Championship football team; by Chadwick Studio*

Pg 143: Don North and prekindergarten kids at Halloween, 2002, by Kim Wind

Pg 152: Class of 2006 flag hanging in the Upper School student lounge, 2005, by Lynn Fort

Pg 160: Mrs. Kinkaid, 1940's, by Rouland*

Back fly sheet: Kinkaid bell created by Pat Foley*

**EVERY ATTEMPT HAS BEEN MADE TO IDENTIFY AND CREDIT ALL PHOTOGRAPHY IN THIS BOOK. WE REGRET ANY ERRORS OR OMISSIONS.**

* Kinkaid archives

THY PRAISES HIG

KINKAID, MY

MY HOMAGE NOW

KINKAID, MY

WITH FRIENDSHIP,

'LL SPREAD MY KNOW

AND HOLD THY PR

KINKAID MY